REAL GRACE
The Teachings of Jesus

Book 1

By
Gregory T. Riether

"Real Grace: The Teachings of Jesus," by Gregory T. Riether. ISBN 978-1-62137-404-6 (Softcover) 978-1-62137-405-3 (eBook)

Library of Congress Number on file with the publisher.

Published 2013 by Virtualbookworm.com Publishing Inc., P.O. Box 9949, College Station, TX 77842, US. ©2013, Gregory T. Riether. All rights reserved. No part of this publication may be reproduced, stored in a retrieval system, or transmitted in any form or by any means, electronic, mechanical, recording or otherwise, without the prior written permission of Gregory T. Riether.

Manufactured in the United States of America.

TABLE OF CONTENTS

PREFACE

The Real Grace series of books, *The Teachings of Jesus*, *The Miracles of Jesus*, and *The Parables of Jesus*, arose from a deep desire to look at the Gospel writings with fresh eyes. I felt compelled to do this for two reasons.

Firstly, my theology of 20 years was seriously shaken by a deeper revelation of grace. The singular concept that all of my sins (past present and future) had all been gathered up by Jesus on the cross and were paid for in their entirety, was something that I had never understood before. God was in Christ reconciling the world (the entire world!) to himself, not counting their sins against them (2 Corinthians 5:17). God is not counting anyone's sins against them! Our religious systems of begging God for forgiveness, however that plays out in every denomination, is anti-Christ. The truth of the gospel is that we have been "perfected forever" (Hebrews 10:14)! Not "perfected until the next time we sin." (Those who want to raise the objection of I John 1:9 should read a succinct little tract by Bob George, *"What About 1 John 1:9."* That verse (that entire first chapter of I John) was not even written to believers.) This is the scandal of the New Covenant in Jesus. "Poor in spirit" people get to inherit the Kingdom! Regarding Jesus and His New Covenant, the only question remaining is, "do you believe this?" Those who believe have eternal life. Those who do not believe are condemned already (John 3:18). Once I received this deeper revelation of Christ's finished work, the Bible opened up to me like never before. It was like having an entirely new Bible! Such joy!

Secondly, I began seeing Jesus for who He was in the Gospel accounts; the transitional figure between the Old Covenant of Law and the New Covenant of Grace. It all seems so elementary now, but at the time, this was a huge revelation. Jesus was always doing one of two things in his ministry; burying people under the demands of the Law of God (in order to get them to give up on their self-efforts at righteousness; i.e. "die to self!") or washing them in the new and living way of Grace (He forgave the lame man's sins without the man confessing, repenting, or even asking for it!). If you don't understand this distinction in Jesus' motives, if you don't understand that the New Covenant was not enacted until Jesus' death, if you don't recognize that much of Jesus' teaching was an attack on the 'Self-effort' system (the Flesh system) you will give equal weight to all the "words in red," believing that they all apply directly to believing Christians. That approach has done grave violence to Jesus' teachings and has kept believers in condemnation and fear. This series of books is an effort to re-capture the powerfully gracious words and ministry of Jesus, and help us see the striking beauty and scandal of "the Word who became flesh, full of grace and truth" (John 1).

As you read through these pages, you will sense a rhythm, at times, in the wording. That is because each of these chapters was preached in my church as a sermon. What you are reading is an edited version of the sermon manuscripts.

I believe these teachings will bless you mightily. I also believe that the Holy Spirit will bear witness in your heart to the truths being presented. Joy to you, my friend. Jesus is SO good! And Papa loves you!

Greg Riether

Introduction

I have split up the words of Jesus into two categories, dedicating a book to each; *The Parables of Jesus* and *The Teachings of Jesus*. In this title, *The Teachings of Jesus*, I wanted to present the most difficult words of Jesus I could find in the four Gospels. Many of these teachings arose from people saying to me, "but Pastor Greg, what about this teaching of Jesus? I don't know how this fits our understanding of Jesus' finished work."

So many of the "what about this teaching" questions come from the Sermon on the Mount. Therefore, that seemed to me to be the place to begin. The Sermon on the Mount is one of the most beloved, one of the most quoted, and one of the most misunderstood passages of scripture. People have used parts of it to bring condemnation on believers and keep believers in fear. After all, didn't Jesus say:

- You must forgive or you won't be forgiven.
- You must be perfect as your heavenly Father is perfect.
- If you are angry with your brother you are in danger of hell fire.
- The way to eternal life is narrow and difficult.
- Every tree that does not bear good fruit is cut down and thrown into the fire.
- If you don't do everything Jesus commands, your house is built on the sinking sand.

The Sermon on the Mount series is one of the most pivotal series of teachings to understand, as Christ's words here in Matthew 5-7 stand as the centerpiece of

Jesus' ministry in the minds of many believers. As you move through these teachings, you will come to a place of great joy as you see the New Covenant unfold before you.

I believe that I at least *touch on* every difficult passage in the gospels and offer the background and framework to understand Jesus' words. The one thing I tell people as they approach our beautiful, compassionate Lord through the gospel writings is, "do not be afraid of ANYTHING Jesus says." For the believer, there is no fear, because His perfect love casts fear out (1 John 4:18). The moment we understand Jesus' context for ministry and his motives in helping people move out of the Flesh System (the Old Covenant Law system) and move into the Spirit System (the New Covenant of Grace) is when His teachings radiate to crystal clarity.

Let us rejoice in the words of our Lord Jesus!

THE SERMON ON THE MOUNT

Part 1 — GIVE UP ON YOUR RIGHTEOUSNESS

What joy when people first receive the message of grace, the true gospel of Jesus! The true gospel of Jesus is that He took all of your sins upon Himself, all your wrongdoings from the beginning of your life to the end of your life, and there is no sin that ever needs paid for again. You are clean and acceptable and given the righteousness of God as a gift forever. You are in a place of son-ship before your Father, and He is pleased with you all the time. You are his beloved son in whom He is well-pleased. God is not counting your sins against you. *"God was in Christ reconciling the world to Himself not counting their sins against them"* (1 Corinthians 5:19). You received that word from Jesus, His gospel over you; He spoke it over you, and you started to receive it and joy just springs up! Life springs up! Love springs up from inside of you and hope that does not disappoint springs up inside of you.

And then people go home and they begin sharing this wonderful message with family and friends, some of whom have grown up in the church and they know the Bible. They hear what you are saying and alarms go off in their head — ding, ding, ding — and they say, "Hey, you're wrong. Sure it says that God perfected you forever, but that can't be what it means. Sure it says you have an eternal redemption, but that can't be what it means. Sure it says God is not counting your sins against you and that you possess the righteousness of God apart from the law, but that can't be what it means." And then they will reach right for words of Jesus from the Sermon on the Mount.

The Sermon on the Mount contains the Lord's Prayer that says, "You have to forgive others or you're not forgiven. And if you marry a divorced person, you are committing adultery. And you have no reward in heaven if you don't store-up your treasures there. And the way to God is narrow and difficult. And everyone who says to me 'Lord, Lord' will enter the kingdom of heaven, but only those who 'do' the will of the Father. And it's the one who does *everything* Jesus said, who is like a man who built his house on the Rock. And if you don't follow through with everything, every command Jesus just gave, you are a person whose house is on sand and great will be your destruction. You can still be destroyed!!!!"

Listen, church, the devil always wants you to turn your eyes back onto your performance and your lack, instead of keeping your eyes firmly on Jesus' performance for you and His supply of grace. But people who do not understand the covenant of grace in Jesus will point to Jesus' Sermon on the Mount; these words of Jesus in red in the red-letter Bibles. I have a friend who used to say, "Read the red and stay on your knees."

Of course, I love everything Jesus said in the gospels. I love His words! And when you understand that Jesus was the transitional figure between the Old Covenant of Law and the New Covenant of Grace, you can interpret Jesus correctly. But if you are mixing the two covenants together, you will misunderstand Jesus. Jesus was introducing a completely new way of relating to God based on grace, based on His finished work. That means a couple of things: number one, it means that He had to get people to see the faultiness of the first covenant of the law. He had to get them to see that their performance was hopelessly lacking. And number two, He had to institute the new covenant of grace, which was enacted at His resurrection. People were not living under the New Covenant until Jesus was raised from the dead. Nobody could have the spirit of Christ indwell them until after the resurrection, really until after Pentecost. So no one was born-again in the entire time of Jesus' earthly ministry. That means that even the faith that people had in Jesus was a self-generated faith, and was different than the faith that born-again believers possess as a gift.

You possess the faith of Jesus, given as a gift. You don't have greater or lesser faith than I do. You were saved by grace through faith, and that faith was a gift of God and not of your works or efforts. Even the stories of faith of people around Jesus who were healed needs to be looked at in light of what the New Covenant of Grace brings to it.

I want to do the impossible. I want to go to the Sermon on the Mount that is so misunderstood by people, and I want to look at the entire Sermon on the Mount, encompassing three chapters in Matthew, and I want to present this overview in a single chapter of this book. I want you to see the heart of Jesus and the strategy of Jesus. So let's begin this overview.

Jesus sat down upon a mountain. The multitudes came. His disciples came. And *"then He opened His mouth and taught them saying"* (Matthew 5:2). The first words out of Jesus' mouth are what we call the "beatitudes." You know what they were in the hearing of these multitudes? They were hope — hope that the kingdom of heaven is within their reach. People who have messed up, people who are poor in spirit, people who know they are unrighteous but who long to be righteous people, people who could never stand a chance based on everything they've been taught about God — Jesus says to them, "The kingdom of heaven belongs to you, you will be comforted, you will inherit the earth, you will be filled with righteousness, you will be pure in heart, you will see God, you will be called sons of God, there is blessing in heaven awaiting you on account of my word."

This is the theme of Jesus' entire ministry. "Repent — the kingdom of heaven is at hand. It is within your reach." Jesus is telling everyday people, who would look at the scribes and Pharisees and their outward righteousness and say to themselves, "Ain't no *way* I have a chance with God." And Jesus starts out the sermon with hope. "Yes, you do stand a chance with God!" In fact, if you are the one who is disqualified, (poor in spirit, longing for righteousness you do not possess) then you got it made, baby! The whole kingdom will belong to you."

The strategy of Jesus is first of all to cast the vision of hope, to strengthen feeble knees. God has a plan for the failed people, and the end result of the plan is that the entire kingdom of God is your possession. That is the intent of God for humanity — this new, impossibly hopeful life. But how does righteousness fill a person, how can a desolate comfortless person receive internal comfort? Something is missing on the inside. Some part of humanity is missing. We are salt that has lost its saltiness. Verse 13 says, *"You are the salt of the earth, but if the salt loses its saltiness, how shall it be seasoned."* There is something intrinsically missing in people; like saltiness missing from salt. The God-intended purpose of our life is affected by this missing ingredient. It is tied to the way we are trying to live life. People are supposed to be lighthouses of God. We are supposed to be such great examples of righteousness that people see our good works and glorify our Father in heaven. They see us, and they praise God and say, "Wow, God, what a blessing that guy is, what a blessing that lady is!"

And now the people listening to Jesus are starting to put their heads down. First, Jesus gave them the hope of the kingdom. But He has to get them to give up the old system of relating to God based on how good they've been, because you are not filled up with righteousness by your doing. You are filled up with righteousness only by receiving it as a gift, by faith, as a child. So He has to get them to see the problem with the way they are approaching God. So, to paraphrase, he says, "People should be singing in the streets about your performance. They should see your good works and praise God." And heads are going down because that is not happening with poor in spirit, righteous-lacking people.

Here is where things heat up. Jesus has to get them to give up on themselves. He has to get them to die to themselves and their efforts at right living. He has to take people, whose entire identity as a nation is tied up in the system of keeping the law of God in order to make God happy, and get them to see the futility of that system and abandon it. Think about it; their entire way of life, their daily life, from the moment these Jewish people got up in the morning until the time when they went to bed at night, was filled with "things you have to do" to stay clean before God. Their daily life, their religious life, and their very identity as a nation are tied to the system of the law. Jesus has to get them to give up on that system. And for the next 31 verses, right to the end of the chapter, Jesus gets more and more brutal; just getting them to look honestly at the failure in this system of the Old Covenant to make them righteous.

Jesus said, "I am not softening the law. I did not come to destroy the law, but to fulfill it. I will do what you have never been able to do." There are those in the crowd who are thinking, "Well, I have kept the law

5

from my youth up," and they start to take offense. Jesus launches an all-out offensive. "Stop fudging! Not a jot or a tittle of the law can be fudged on." The jot is the Hebrew "*yod*," the smallest Hebrew letter, which looks like a little apostrophe. The "tittle" is the little decorative flourish at the end of a letter, a little horn or seraph. Jesus is calling them on their fudging of the law. "You cannot fudge on even the tiniest part of the law."

Look at verse 19: *"Whoever therefore breaks one of the least of these commandments and teaches men so, shall be called least in the kingdom of heaven and whoever does and teaches them, he shall be called great in the kingdom of heaven."* This is heaven's perspective, heaven's opinion of people trying to keep the law. If you so much as break the tiniest part of the law, in the kingdom of heaven they will call you *"elachistos;"* it's a superlative word. It means utterly the lowest thing in existence. "If you mess up on the tiniest part of the law, heaven judges you as the least-worthy creature ever created. That is heaven's opinion of you. Of course, if you do it all right, then heaven considers you the greatest of all. Yeah, how is heaven judging you?"

Under the law system, you only have two options: you are either perfect as your heavenly Father is perfect and are greatest in the kingdom of heaven *or* you are the least and lowest, deserving of wrath. Because Jesus came to fulfill the law for you, when you came to believe on Him, He gave you His righteousness, His perfection, and you became (at that moment and forever) the greatest in the kingdom of heaven. But you see, under the law covenant, everybody falls under one of those two categories.

"For I say to you that unless your righteousness exceeds (*'perisseuo'* — to super-abound, super-

abounds beyond) *the righteousness of the scribes and Pharisees, you will by no means enter the kingdom of heaven"* (Verse 20). Jesus is not being mean, He is getting them to give up. "Please give up. Please see that you need another way. I will be that way, a new and living way." That is His heart. And in this whole next section, Jesus just intensifies the burden of the law. He literally buries them in the demands of the law to get them to give up and die to self-effort.

"You have heard that it was said, 'Do not murder. I say if you are even angry, you are in danger of hellfire.'" Anger is murder. Lusting is the same as adultery. "If you have married a divorced person, you have committed adultery." Is anyone left standing yet? Then let me continue. "If your right arm offends you, cut it off; if your eye causes you to sin, gouge it out." That's how serious the offense is. That's the law. Are you sons of the law? Are you living by the Red Words of Jesus? If you are taking these words as a new law that we are now to live under, Jesus made it harder for you. Go ahead and live by the words in red. Time to quit being a hypocrite and take that steak knife and start sawing off your hands and gouging out your eyes. You can't do it, that's the point. Just agree with Jesus — the old system doesn't work. You have hopelessly broken the law.

Right in the middle of this, Jesus has His little parable. *"Agree with your Adversary quickly, while you are on the way with him"* (Verse 25). The adversary is Satan. In fact, Peter uses this exact word to describe our adversary who walks about as a roaring lion. The adversary is the accuser. Satan wants you to feel rejected by God. Jesus is saying here that while you are on the way with him, while you are on earth, just agree quickly with him. "I've blown it, and I need a new way to God."

And then Jesus delves back into the law. He looks up to see if anyone is still standing, and He keeps going. "Are you taking an oath, is your mouth jabbering away? Your oaths are an offense. If anything more than "yes" or "no" is coming out of your mouth, it is from the evil one." How about that? Baby, I am on a roll. "If your enemy sues you, just give him more than he asks for. If he punches you in the face, tell him it's okay to punch the other side of your face, for that is the fulfillment of the law. You think you can hate your enemy; no, you must love your enemy. Bless those who curse you, pray favor on those who harm you, that you may be sons of your Father in heaven" (verse 45).

What makes you a son under this system? *Doing it all!* But if you omit one jot or tittle, heaven judges you as the lowest of the low. And the very climax of this section of the Sermon is verse 48: *"Therefore you shall be perfect, just as your Father in heaven is perfect."*

People are left speechless. Listen, do not let people pull verses from this section and bring you under condemnation. The whole section is meant to condemn *everyone* so we would give up on ourselves. Jesus does not want you living in condemnation. He just wants us to be honest about the system we are using to relate to God. If it's the law system, if God is pleased or angry at you based on how well you've kept the law, then you are righteously-challenged and that condemnation that you are living under will kill you. It will make you crazy. Some of the most messed-up people I've seen were people who came out of good Christian homes, where the law of God was the system they lived under and they ate nothing but guilt for breakfast, lunch, and dinner. There is a better way and His name is Jesus, which means "Yahweh saves." *He* saves. *You* don't save. *He does*. Relax in His saving work. You are forgiven and free, living under His marvelous grace.

At this point in the Sermon on the Mount, Jesus softens His approach. He begins an appeal to the everyday people, and He keeps helping them to see the difficulty of the system they are living under; it's a system of conditional rewards. In fact, I call this section in chapter 6 the "Conditional Blessings Under the Law System." And I'm going to tell you something that makes people mad. This section does not apply directly to believers. I'm not saying that there aren't some principles for living that the Holy Spirit will lead you into, there is truth in that; practicing your charitable deeds without fanfare and so forth. But again, Jesus is talking to people under the Old Covenant of the law, and getting them to see how difficult it is so they will give up on it. The one word used throughout this section is the word "reward" (*misthon*) which means "earned wages." You are not under the system of earned wages.

"Take heed that you do not do your charitable deeds before men, to be seen by them. Otherwise you have no reward from your Father in heaven" (chapter 6:1). I heard a pastor say that sometimes he lets his congregation see his financial giving so that he will be an example to them, even though (he said) he loses his reward in heaven for that gift when he does that. No! Listen, this will upset some people, but you do not have a bank account in heaven that you make deposits into. I've heard every screwy theology out there, and one of them is that you can make deposits in heaven with your tithes or your good works, and then you can make withdrawals on that account. No! Stop, stop! That whole thing is Old Covenant works that earn God's blessing.

As a believer, you already possess every spiritual blessing in the heavenlies. The whole "storing up treasure in heaven," storing up coupons redeemable for God's favor at a later date — that is Old Covenant stuff. Jesus says, in this sermon, to get your eyes off of mammon and get your eyes on your treasure. You, friends, have your treasure in earthen vessels. Jesus your treasure is in you. You carry Him with you. You don't need Old Covenant redeemable coupons. You possess the treasure. It is in you. And everything you need has been given in Christ. You don't need to beg God for forgiveness, you don't need to beg Him for daily bread, and you don't need to beg Him to protect you from the evil one. You don't need to beg Him for His kingdom to come. It has already come! *It is in you!* *"For the kingdom of God is not eating and drinking, but righteousness and peace and joy in the Holy Spirit"* (Romans 14:17).

The Lord's Prayer is an Old Covenant prayer of conditional blessing. If you forgive men, God will forgive you. I've heard so many bad sermons by pastors trying to *make* the theology of the Lord's Prayer fit the New Covenant. And you get these whacked out ideas that if you as a believer don't forgive men their trespasses, it's not that God *really* won't forgive you (even though Jesus says that); it's just that He won't be in fellowship with you." Stop the insanity. Look at what Jesus is doing. He's showing them the futility of the Old Covenant system.

At the end, people are saying, "What can we possibly do? We are failed servants of God." Just as they get to the point of despair under the Law Covenant, Jesus gives them the key to receiving from God. To me, this is the high point, the climax, the Mount Everest of the Sermon on the Mount. And it changes everything. He is talking about human needs and how people make the mistake of focusing on money or focusing on human needs — "what shall we eat or what shall we drink" as the purpose for living, as the goal to be attained. "No," Jesus says, "here is the goal, here is what's missing. This is the saltiness of salt, this is the fulfillment of the law; everything flows from this."

"But seek first the kingdom of God and His righteousness, and all these things will be added to you" (Matthew 6:33). "Seek the kingdom of God" — in other words, discern what God is doing; discern this new thing, seek the kingdom of God and *His* righteousness, not *your* righteousness. Don't seek the establishment of *your* right living. Seek the very righteousness that God is in possession of. Look for *God's* righteousness. Everything else will be added to you when you find that; everything else will fall into place. For "*those who receive abundance of grace and the gift of righteousness will reign in life*" (Romans 5:17). That's referring to this life, right here on earth.

A shift in our thinking is needed. "*Judge not that you be not judged, for with what judgment you judge, you will be judged*" (Matthew 7:1). If you live by the law, then you will judge people by the law. That is a faulty system. *"Why do you look at the speck in your brother's eye, but do not consider the plank in your own eye"* (verse 3)? The word "plank" is the word "*dokos*;" it's a beam of wood. It literally means "to hold up." Jesus is talking about a foundation beam. You have got to get rid of the foundation beam that's stuck in your eye, pull the foundation beam out, and let that whole system of the flesh collapse in on itself. Then you will see clearly.

What is it we are supposed to see clearly? What does this relationship with God really look like? If the system of serving God is hopelessly broken, what can be put in its place? Jesus gives it to you, and He is making a total paradigm shift. Here is the radical new way with God. It's not you working to serve a distant and angry deity. It's you seeing your place in His family. He is a daddy who loves you, and He sees you as His little child. And He knows what you need. He attends to you in absolute love and nothing else. Verse 11: "If you being evil know how to give good gifts to your children, how much more will your Father in heaven give good things to those who *"work hard and do everything right before Him*?" No! *To those who ask.* The gift comes out of the heart of love of a Father, not on your performance in holy living!

Jesus ends it this way: "If you can receive this new paradigm, you have built your house on a Rock, and that Rock is Jesus. And if your house is built on a Rock, it's just as if you heard and obeyed every single saying that I have just given you." Jesus said, "These two statements are an equal equation — hearing and doing every single thing I've said in this parable, *and* building your house on a rock." If your house is built on Jesus alone, and not your efforts, it's the same as fulfilling everything that Jesus just spoke. You are perfect as your heavenly Father is perfect. And the naysayers and the storms of life and the accuser of the brethren and the people who will beat on your house and pummel your house of faith accusing you of all manner of things; *that storm* will blow on you, but you will be unshakable because the Rock is solid.

Anchor yourself in the finished work of Jesus, and let *no one* pour any other word into you other than the word of grace. Jesus has qualified you. Jesus is your rescuer forever. Jesus forgave all your sin and settled the sin issue. No matter what you do or don't do, the kingdom of heaven judges you "great!" You are the greatest in the kingdom. You are filled up with righteousness. The kingdom of heaven belongs to you. You have obtained mercy. You are seeing God. You are called sons of God. Now get out there and inherit the earth. It belongs to you. Because you sought the kingdom of God and found His righteousness, every other thing you need has been given to you. That's Jesus. That's your Savior. Hallelujah!!

THE SERMON ON THE MOUNT

Part 2 — JUDGE NOT: OF MOTES AND BEAMS

Jesus has been burying the people under the Old Covenant law, getting them to see the impossibilities of living under that covenant. And kind, loving Jesus makes Himself the mouthpiece for the law of God, and the words that He speaks are as brutal as the Law of God because people have made the law doable; they have weakened it. Jesus is trying to get them to see the fallacy of the law system, the Law Covenant; that it is not a good deal for them, that God finds fault with this system. It needs replaced with something that only He can give you.

And then He begins to introduce the replacement for that system. The new system is not like the old. The new system, the New Covenant is not getting your master God to bless you, His servant. It is God, (your Daddy, your Abba, your Papa) who loves you, (His daughter, His son), and He sees your needs, all of them, even your need for righteousness. *"For your heavenly Papa knows that you need all these things"* (verse 32) and He gives you what you need as a father gives good things to his precious children. "You just seek first the kingdom of God and His righteousness and all these things shall be added unto you." Stop seeking your own righteousness. Seek instead the righteousness that only God possesses, His own righteousness that He will give to you freely as a gift.

Now that is a new system. Your faith in Jesus makes you a partaker. He gives you His righteousness and He qualifies you, perfects you in your spirit, eternally redeems you, and puts you in the grip of His hand and nothing can take you from His grip. That means no power on earth, no scheme of the devil, no amount of messing up on your part, no amount of failure, or disobedience or sin can take you from His grip!

He remembers you and keeps you even when you don't remember Him. He does this because He is a father and a good father can never forget his kids even if they ignore him, He will not ignore you. *"Can a woman forget her nursing child and not have compassion on the son of her womb? Surely they may forget, yet I will not forget you."* Like the prodigal, you can sleep with the swine and spend out wastefully what He gives you, but you remain His son! And when you come to your senses and come back to talk to your Papa, He doesn't want to hear your mess-ups. He is so far past that; those were paid for in Christ. He just wants to remind you of who you are and lavish love on you and remind you of who you have always been — His son! He wants to put the robe on you and make your life easier to walk with His shoes and put the ring of authority back on your hand, as a reminder of your identity. Friends, if you've been away from God in your mind and you've come back home today, listen to me, God is not mad at you. He was never mad at you! Never!

That is the power of Christ's finished work upon you. He takes care of the sin issue, so that you can always and forever be in a position of love and "no condemnation." *"There is now no condemnation for those who are in Christ"* (Romans 8:1). And that just changes everything. It changes how you see God, it changes how you see yourself, and it changes how you see others. Part of what Jesus preached in the Sermon on the Mount has to do with how we see others, both under the Law Covenant (the law that spies out our disobedience — if you are a son of the law, you are doing the law's bidding — spying out disobedience in others), and under the New Covenant that "spies out the righteousness of Jesus."

"Judge not, that you be not judged. For with what judgment you judge, you will be judged, and with the measure you use; it will be measured back to you" (Matthew 7:1). Now Jesus is really talking about two different ideas here that always go together — the judgment and the measurement. A judgment is a declaration of guilt or innocence. And the measurement is the standard by which you make a judgment of guilt or innocence. If you are looking at someone to judge them, you have (in your mind) some measuring device or standard that you are using. If you are judging them *by their actions*, you are giving either approval or condemnation based on your standard of measurement (which is your interpretation of the Law of God). Jesus has just spent two entire chapters telling us how our standard of measurement using the Law of God is totally jacked up.

We might *say* that our standard, (our measurement) is "God's standard in His law, the Law of Moses," but Jesus says that we are not reading that measurement right. We are fudging on it with ourselves, we are making it doable, we are using it to establish our own righteousness in our minds, and nothing good is going to come out of that delusion. Stop fudging, and stop judging. Because if you are using God's measuring standard of the law correctly, the only judgment that can ever come out of it is the judgment of guilty. You are guilty. And those who judge by the law of God, those who are living under that burdensome system, are experts in seeing the guilt in other people and experts on fudging it when it comes to themselves. They see themselves as experts in cleaning up *your* life and getting *your* life right with God. "I will judge you, using the measuring rod of God's Mosaic law under the Old Covenant, and I will see your faults and then I will help you get your life together by telling you how to act better so that God will be pleased."

Jesus said that kind of person is like a man who looks for the speck in someone's eye, but does not consider the plank in their own eye. Verses 4-5: *"Or how can you say to your brother, 'Let me remove the speck from your eye; and look, a plank is in your own eye.' Hypocrite! First remove the plank from your own eye, and then you will see clearly to remove the speck from your brother's eye."* People relating to God using the measuring rod of the law don't even know what the speck is that they are seeing in their brother's eye. They think that it's some sin that they need to clean up. But it isn't "a" sin that they need to clean up.

About a year ago, I was with Sherry and our little granddaughter in our back yard. It was evening and starting to get dark, and we were just running around having fun. I ran right into this low lying branch of one of our trees, and this little branch poked me right in my open eye. Ouch! I mean, ouch! I came in and washed the eye out and tried to make it feel better. But it was not feeling better. I tried going to bed, but the pain was unbearable. Finally, Sherry took me to the emergency room and the doctor flushed it out. It turns out I had a mote in my eye. Hey, this is a biblical injury. This is the Bible come to life because the word for "mote," translated as "speck" here, literally means "tiny, dry twig." They washed it out, put some medicine on it, and I blessed that doctor.

But here's my point: I could not do anything with that thing in my eye. I tried to help out with some things, but my whole world was tied up with this mote, this speck. I was completely preoccupied with it. The baseline pain was unrelenting and unbelievable. I could not stop holding my eye, praying for relief. My life was literally put on hold with my preoccupation with this. That is what a mote is in a person's eye. The mote that Jesus is talking about, the mote (speck in the eye) that is such a horrible, all-consuming irritant, the mote that keeps people preoccupied and unable to function in life, the mote that is embedded in our eye that clouds our vision, is the Law of God itself, and when the Law of God is in your vision, it brings an all-consuming irritation called "condemnation."

The Apostle Paul said that all that is of hay and stubble will be burned up in the final judgment (that's the mote!). He meant anything having to do with human effort to get right or stay right with God will be burned up — everything not of grace, everything not of Jesus. Because when the Law of God, even a little bit of it, is in your eye, it is enough to cause great condemnation.

Even irreligious people, who do not understand Jesus and His grace (they carry motes with them) — even they know that they have failed God, and they know that they are unqualified for the right to His blessings. They come to God (if at all) in uncertainty and tentativeness hoping God is not mad at them, hoping God (by His love) can see past their failures. Their condemnation (under a law that they know *by instinct*) is governing how they come to God. What do they need? They need a mote emergency room doctor. They need the law removed. The problem is that typical Christianity isn't good at mote removal. If the religious doctor (expert) is under the Old Covenant, trying to please God by their own actions and is really examining themselves and sin focused, looking inward, trying to come to a place of peace with God by the strict doing of the law, *they* have more condemnation in them than the person they are trying to save who is not religious.

The irony of it all is that the more religious you are the bigger the irritant; the more religious you are, the more incompetent you are at mote removal. Jesus said this of the law keepers, the Pharisees, who were as good as you could get at keeping the law: *"Woe to you, scribes and Pharisees, hypocrites! For you travel land and sea to win one proselyte, and when he is won, you make him twice as much a son of hell as yourselves"* (Matthew 23:15). You make him hardened into the law system. You take the big foundation beam of the law that is in your eye and you stick it in his eye, and you think you've solved the problem. Religious people mis-diagnose the mote; they think it's some little sin that they have to clean up to get right with God. And all along they do not understand that what this other person really needs (and what *they themselves* desperately need) is for their eyes to be washed out with the word of grace! Grace washes out the law, so that the horrible pain of condemnation is alleviated.

Besides the law, there is another measuring standard, the one that God uses. It is the Word of the Kingdom, the Word that came down from heaven; Jesus, full of grace and truth. Truth is on the side of grace. Believe God's grace in Jesus. It is truth! In fact, Jesus speaks this teaching a little differently in Mark 4:24-25. Jesus uses the same word here for measure, as He does in Matthew 7. *"Then He said to them, 'Take heed what you hear; with the same measure you use, it will be measured to you, and to you who hear, more will be given. For whoever has, to him more will be given; but whoever does not have, even what he has will be taken away.'"*

What is the measuring standard you want applied to you? What should you *"do unto others"* that you also want them to *"do to you?"* Give them grace! Grace in Jesus is the fulfillment of the law and the prophets. It is the word of the Kingdom that comes through hearing. It is the word of Jesus, the word of grace. When you receive that word for yourself, you just naturally start giving that word out to others.

You live by the word of grace when your daily walk becomes the confession of "Jesus took my sins, and I am acceptable and free and innocent and qualified for blessings." When your daily walk is "I am loved and free and God is not holding any of my sins against me," then you are one who has, and more will be given. Pity the person who does not "have" that; even what they have will be taken away. The devil will steal it, because the mote, the law, the irritant of condemnation, occupies their life and they have no confidence before God to ask in faith for anything. They are constantly confessing their sin, and they have no authority. They wonder about God's love for them, they wonder about whether they've been good enough for heaven, and on and on.

But when your eyes are flushed out by the word of grace and when the irritant and preoccupation of condemnation is washed out by grace, when the law is out of your vision, then you can see clearly. And *that* is when you are qualified to remove the motes from other people. You have stopped judging them on the basis of the law, and you see them using the measuring standard of God's grace. And so you can go up to people you are just having casual conversation with and say, "Man, God wants you to you know that He is not holding anything against you — nothing. He loves you right now; before you do anything. That's what Jesus did for you. Believe it!" And what comes out of that statement to that person is true faith if they are in any way open.

I have not had any irreligious person, not a single one that I have spoken that to, not be positively affected by that statement. People are so hungry for the gift of "no condemnation," the gift that Jesus gives, that when you speak it out, they sense the truth of it and the power of it. Of course, I have had plenty of *religious* people get mad at me, which is why Jesus said, *"Don't take what is holy* (holy means "weird," unearthly like God, i.e. grace) *and give it to the dogs; don't cast your pearls before swine lest they trample them under their feet, and turn and tear you in pieces"* (verse 6). Religious people relating to God by their own efforts hate this word of grace. And they want to bury it, trample it under their feet. And when they are done trampling the Gospel of Jesus, they'll turn on you and use the law on you and heap condemnation on your life, tearing you up one side and down the other.

I would much rather talk to irreligious people, in just everyday work life or wherever, who have no expectation of a word of grace from God to be spoken over them. Because when you speak it out, they know they are hearing heaven, and it changes people forever. When you finally "get" the good news of Jesus' finished work in you, then your measuring standard changes altogether. And friends, especially with believers, we need to apply this measuring standard to our brothers and sisters in the faith.

In 2 Corinthians 10:7, Paul is talking about how his brothers and sisters in Corinth view him. How do they judge him? And he uses in this verse, the exact same word that Jesus used in Matthew 7. *"Do you look at things according to the outward appearance?"*

What is that? Judging a person on the basis of what you can see them doing with your eyes. Are you judging them according to their actions of right or wrong living? Are you judging them according to the outward appearance?

"If anyone is convinced in himself that he is Christ's, let him again consider this in himself, that just as he is Christ's, even so we are Christ's." In other words, "if you get the idea that you belong to Christ forever, it is by His grace and His beautiful work." If you understand that you are Christ's possession and He is working things out in you, then you need to practice seeing other believers as Christ's possession and know that He is also working things out in them, just as patiently as He is working them out in you. This gospel of grace is changing people from the inside out, even if you can't see it.

This is St. Paul's whole argument in verse 3: *"For though we walk in the flesh, we do not war according to the flesh."* In other words, even though we are in flesh bodies, we don't do battle against sin using our own strength, using the flesh system of bucking up and trying to fly right by our own determination and willpower. That would be doing battle according to the flesh. *"For the weapons of our warfare are not carnal but mighty in God for pulling down strongholds, casting down arguments and every high thing that exalts itself against the knowledge of God, bringing every thought into captivity to the obedience of Christ"* (verse 4).

This is talking about the power of the Gospel of Jesus Christ, the word of grace. This *"knowledge of God"* is the way God does warfare. And this gospel is so powerful that it can pull down every unrighteous stronghold in a person. Everything in every believer that is working contrary to God, every stronghold in every believer is being defeated by the gospel of grace. That is happening in you right now. How does it work? It works by bringing *every thought into captivity to the obedience of Christ*.

When I used to read that verse in my former life as a Pharisee, I thought, "Okay, I just had a bad thought, a sinful thought, I need to get that thought into obedience. I need to come against it like Christ would; I need to see that thought for what it is and bring it into captivity, bring it into obedience and stop thinking that way." Stop it. Just stop! No, that is warfare according to my own strength, according to the flesh.

How do you do warfare according to the spirit? You see that thought for what it is, and bring it into captivity to the obedience of Christ. *The obedience of Christ is Christ's obedience, not mine.* The obedience of Christ is His finished work that He did in me and for me. I have some stronghold thought or pattern of thinking in my mind and I see it for what it is, and instead of coming under condemnation and fighting it by my strength, I remember that Jesus has that thought covered right there, right now, by His finished work, by His grace, and that thought has no dominion over me at all.

Jesus is working His grace into the minds of His people, and they are being transformed by the renewing of their minds, more and more and more. And here's the thing, you can't see that. It is not an outward action that can be judged. It is an inward working of the spirit of grace in a person. We don't know all that Jesus in doing in people. It is absolutely wrong to judge someone according to outward appearance, according to the law, according to your understanding of right and wrong, according to where *you* think *they* ought to be in their walk with God.

Paul says, "You just remember that they are completely in Christ like you are completely in Christ and let's let Christ and the Holy Spirit have all the elbow room they need to pull down strongholds in people. For we judge no man according to the flesh any longer. We have a different measuring standard; it's the same one that got applied to *our* life and that measuring standard is: Grace! Grace! Grace!!" I have confidence that the Holy Spirit is bringing down strongholds in us. Jesus is at work in people to replace flakiness or unfaithfulness or a foul-mouth or every other unrighteousness behavior. He is at work in people. And the Holy Spirit is a patient worker in people. You have received the gift of "no condemnation," and that is what we get to give out. Freely we have received. Freely give.

Here is the reason we do not judge others. In the new system, God has already declared the judgment over you, based on the new measuring standard. What is the measuring standard? The measuring standard of Jesus is "Grace." And the judgment on you is "innocent." And that's some good news!

THE SERMON ON THE MOUNT

Part 3 — ASK AND IT WILL BE GIVEN

Keeping the Law Covenant to get God's approval and attention and gain access to heaven is the wide road, the broad way that leads to certain destruction because it is impossible. But Jesus came to introduce a new way — a way that is through Him alone. It is only Jesus, so that this new way is narrow. *"Narrow is the gate and difficult is the way which leads to life, and there are few who find it"* (verse 14). That word for "difficult" literally means "crowded out." Young's Literal translation says, *"How strait is the gate, and compressed is the way that is leading to the life."*

The way is not difficult (as in striving hard); it is compressed, it is crowded out, it is choked out by the system of relating to God that *everybody* uses. Karma, do good — get good, your efforts, trying harder to please God, trying to get God to like you, trying to get God to bless you by doing good, trying to keep from going to hell by not doing too many bad things. All these things are what crowds it out. That is the broad way that everyone takes. That is the path that leads to your destruction.

Jesus is introducing to us, in the Sermon on the Mount, a new way. It is a way where the kingdom of God is accessible to ordinary people ("blessed are the poor in spirit, for theirs is the kingdom of heaven" — access to God and heaven for the spiritual mess-ups). It is a way that is not dependent on your performance in keeping the law, *but is dependent on His performance in keeping the law for you.* Jesus said, "I came to fulfill the law! I am its fulfillment." It is the narrow way, the way to life.

Do you see that Jesus is lifting up two approaches to God here — the narrow and crowded out way versus the broad and wide way. It's not the "sin way" versus the "no sin way." It is two different covenants, two entirely different life-approaches. Your efforts at righteousness are doomed to fail — could Jesus have made that any clearer than the Sermon on the Mount? That is the way of conditional blessings, pleading to God for forgiveness that is based on you being able to forgive others, and begging Him for necessities every day. That is the one approach; that is the broad and wide way everyone takes, even most believers!

What is the other way? Jesus gave them a little taste in chapter 5. It involves seeking *God's own* righteousness as a gift, given to you — not *your* righteousness. Jesus said that to them, then He said, "Oh, this is holy, what I'm telling you. It's so holy and different, that religious people won't like it. If you try to tell religious people about it, they'll trample it under foot and then turn on you and tear you up."

The holy way, the new way of God works like this: *"Ask and it will be given to you* (what has He been talking about? — righteousness!); *seek, and you will find; knock, and it will be opened to you. For everyone who asks receives, and he who seeks finds, and to him who knocks it will be opened. Or what man is there among you who, if his son asks for bread, will give him a stone? Or if he asks for a fish, will he give him a serpent? If you then, being evil, know how to give good gifts to your children, how much more will your Father who is in heaven give good things to those who ask Him!"* (Matthew 7:7-11) How does righteousness come through Jesus, the bread of life? If a son asks for bread (asks for righteousness in Jesus), will the Father give him a stone? If you ask for righteousness in Jesus, is God going to give you another tablet of stone (more commandments, more stuff to do)? No, He is going to satisfy you.

Look at the first part of this. *"Ask, and it will be given."* We are to seek the kingdom of God and His righteousness. How do we get it? Ask, and it will be given. Jesus uses three words here: "ask, seek, and knock." And He links a second word to each of these words. Ask — given. Seek — you will find. Knock, it will be opened. "Ask-given, seek-find, knock-opened." And then He repeats these in verse 8, with one change. Verse 8: "For everyone who asks receives, and he who seeks finds, and to him who knocks it will be opened." "Seek-and find" are the same. "Knock — opened" are the same. But the "ask and given" have changed to *"ask-receive."*

He says, *"Ask and it will be given."* Ask for God's righteousness and God will give it to you. But just so you know that it doesn't get lost in the shipping, verse 8 says, *"For everyone who asks, receives."* God doesn't just give it on His end. He makes sure you receive it on your end. For everyone who asks, receives.

Now that's beautiful, but how can that be? Jesus is introducing a new thing here. This is a totally new paradigm. It's not you, the servant of the Lord, trying to get something out of God, your master, the hard taskmaster who is waiting to thump you for sin. The new paradigm is: "God is a Father caring for you, His child." Now this is so incredible, this shift is so far removed from their normal thinking, that Jesus only gave them bite sized portions to chew on. This is His introduction to a New Covenant. And when He spoke this same teaching again, He added another parable to help them get this concept and Luke recorded this. You see this same teaching in Luke 11:9-11: *"Ask and it will be given to you; seek, and you will find. For everyone who asks, receives. If a son asks for bread from any father among you, will he give him a stone?"*

This is a re-telling (by Jesus) of illustrations He used on the Sermon on the Mount, so the point He is making is the same. He is lifting up two approaches (or ways) to God — the wide, broad way that leads to destruction versus the narrow, crowded-out way that leads to eternal life.

But look at how he compares these two ways. He is using parallelism. At the beginning of chapter 11 with this teaching, you have the Lord's Prayer, which is an Old Covenant prayer. The Lord's Prayer is for people still under the Law Covenant. I listened to a Jewish scholar who was teaching on prayer, a practicing Jew who said that any good Jew could pray the Lord's Prayer. It is a prayer of conditional blessings.

Jesus speaks out this Old Covenant prayer, and then gives a parable to describe life with God under that prayer. It is like you trying to get something out of a sleeping God: *"Which of you shall have a friend, and go to him at midnight and say to him, 'Friend, lend me three loaves'"* (verse 5). You are the friend going to God, asking for loaves. What is God's response to your request? *"And he will answer from within and say, 'Do not trouble me, the door is now shut, and my children are with me in bed; I cannot rise and give to you? I say to you, though he will not rise and give to him because he is his friend, yet because of his persistence he will rise and give him as many as he needs'"* (verses 7-8).

This is God's goodness under the Old Covenant of the Law, the covenant of "do good, get good; do bad, get bad." People operating under that covenant with God have messed it up; they have failed on their end.

They haven't kept up their friendship with God. God is not impressed with the friendship in this parable. He is not moved to action because of the friendship. But because the guy is good at pestering God, God, in his goodness will give him what he needs. So you see, it's an Old Covenant prayer (Lord's Prayer), followed by a parable of life under the Old Covenant (which was life as a Jew in Jesus' day).

Then Jesus does it again. He introduces a model of prayer under a different covenant (just like before), then He tells you in parable form of what that model is like in contrast to the first model. The first model is: you are on the outside, the door is closed, it's an inconvenience for God, and you pester, pester, pester. If you pester enough, then God, by His goodness, will honor your request because He is so good, not because your relationship with Him is so good.

The *new* model of prayer is: ask and it will be given by God, and He will even make sure you receive it. Seek and you will find. Knock and doors will fly open to you. For *everyone* in this model receives and finds and gets doors kicked open. Why? How can that be? Here's the parable: *It's a son asking from daddy, not an estranged friend asking at inconvenient times!* It's even better than that. You are not the estranged friend, whose friendship does not move God to action. You are not the estranged friend who is on the other side of the shut door, the other side of the locked door. The door is *not* shut between you and God. *You are the child who is curled up with Daddy in bed* ("*my children are with me in bed*"). The homes in Jesus' day were not like the homes we have today, where we have a different room for everything. The homes of common everyday people in Jesus' day had two rooms — an inner room and an outer room.

When we were in Israel, we drove up to the northern part of the Sea of Galilee and actually saw the remains of the town of Capernaum. Capernaum was Jesus' home base of ministry. That's where Peter lived, in his mother-in-law's house. Peter's house is there, what's left of it. It is a "triple A rated, verified, this is the house" kind of site. Put up a sign, "Jesus slept here." Like, not just in this vicinity, but right here. You've got twelve disciples sleeping there. It would have been wall to wall snoring fisherman. It's no wonder Jesus went off to a lonely place by Himself. You would have too!

But a family in Jesus' day would have a single pallet that they would all sleep on in the main room, all of them together. Now get this image in your head. The God figure in the first parable is saying to the estranged friend, *"Do not trouble me, the door is now shut, and my children are with me in bed."* That's Old Covenant. You are the estranged friend, begging from the other side of the shut and locked door. But, what is the New Covenant like? Jesus said it is the son asking the Father for what he needs. Do you see the switch that Jesus has made? In the New Covenant, you are *not* the estranged friend on the other side of the door. You are the son, curled up in bed with your Daddy. You are on the inside with Dad!

Son-ship! That is the basis of the New Covenant in Jesus! Not estrangement. It's not you having to prove your friendship with God. You're there, man! You're right there with Him on the inside. He's got His arms around you and you are protected and you have got everything you need. And if you want anything else, just ask! Ask — it will be given to you. And you will receive. This is what Jesus came to give you — son-ship in the family *and* the inheritance that goes with it.

"But when the fullness of the time had come, God sent forth His Son, born of a woman, born under the law, to redeem those who were under the law, that we might receive the adoption as sons. And because you are sons, God has sent forth the Spirit of His Son into your hearts, crying out, 'Abba, Father!' Therefore you are no longer a slave but a son, and if a son, then an heir of God through Christ" (Galatians 4:4-7). Jesus redeemed you from servant-hood. You are no longer a servant. On the night of Jesus' betrayal and arrest, His last night of earthly ministry, He said to His disciples, *"No longer do I call you servants, for a servant does not know what his master is doing"* (John 15).

Now that is a new mark in their relationship. It is no longer servant/master, or slave/ master. This is important. Jesus demarcated that moment for us. That means that every parable Jesus told (before that) that speaks of servant-hood before God needs to be re-looked at and reevaluated based on a new covenant. When I die and go stand before Papa, I'm not looking for the words *"well done, good and faithful servant."* I don't want to hear that. Do not put that on the bulletin covers of my funeral. I'm not a servant; I am a son! When I go to Papa at the end of my life I want to hear, "Welcome home, son!"

Jesus redeemed you from servant-hood. And now you possess the Spirit by which you cry out "Abba, Daddy." And the inheritance belongs to you. *"And if a son, an heir of God through Christ"* (verse 7). An heir is one who receives an inheritance. An inheritance is what you get upon the death of the one who has all the goods. Jesus said, "All things that the Father has are mine." Now this is the inheritance. The Father possesses all things. He gave all things to the Son. And Jesus, the Son said, "I leave it all to you — all things." And when Jesus died, the inheritance was enacted, and you now (the poor in spirit) have an inheritance. What is it? *All things. All things!*

Ask, and it will be given, and you will receive. The only problem is in getting people to believe this. We have to abandon all of the models of prayer that we were taught before, like people using prayer to "get close" to God. No, the Holy Spirit has been given as the executor of the inheritance and He is *in* you.

If you ask for something that you need and you wonder if God heard you or if you will receive it, just turn and look at the deposit of the Spirit that is in you and who is your guarantee of the inheritance. When you doubt, just begin saying, "The Spirit is in me. It is Christ's own Spirit inhabiting my frame." He inhabits your frame. He inhabits every believer's frame. He is the guarantor, the executor of the inheritance. Everything you ask for, the Holy Spirit is the answer because He executes the inheritance. Since He is inside of you as the executor of the inheritance, you can ask and know that it is given, and you will receive. How different from the Old Covenant!

Get rid of all the prayer manuals you've read in the past. Get rid of all of that punching holes in the heavenlies for the blessings to come down and all of the stuff based on Old Testament examples or based on Old Covenant persistence parables; it is not for you. Prayer is not the way to close the gap between you and God, it's not the way to get the windows of heaven to open, and it's not the way to get God to open the door for you. You have to get that image out of your head. And you have to know who *you* are, and you have to know who *God* is. You are not the estranged friend on the outside; you are curled up in bed right next to Papa. So Ask! Ask! Ask! This is the New Covenant! The inheritance belongs to you. Jesus purchased it and gave it to you. It's easy. But you have to get the image out

32

of your head that you are the servant, you are the estranged friend, and God is some distant deity/master in heaven on the other side of the door. And I can guarantee you that this is the greatest obstacle to our joy. We see ourselves wrongly.

I have a teaching about Mephibosheth in the Old Testament that just describes so many believers. Mephibosheth was a man who had nothing. He was the grandson of slain King Saul. But David wanted to honor him and he picked up Mephibosheth from Lodebar, from his poverty, and David brought him to his own house and gave to him all the land and possessions that King Saul had possessed. And in an instant, Mephibosheth went from being a pauper and an outcast in the land to being the second wealthiest person in Israel, with the rights to dine every day at the King's table. That is a parable of a believer. That is what Jesus does the moment you *ask* Him to come in. He is given and you receive. You are set down right in the middle of your inheritance. But we don't believe it.

The problem was that Mephibosheth never did get comfortable in that position. Externally, Mephibosheth's position and standing had changed 180 degrees. But internally, *Mephibosheth had such a hard time making the transition because he never saw himself as worthy.* In fact, Mephibosheth called himself a "dead dog." That was his opinion of himself — a lowly dog of a man, who does not even merit life. Mephibosheth was lame in his legs, probably paralyzed, because when he was five years old his nurse maid was running with him in her arms and she tripped and out flew Mephebosheth and he landed and broke his back. He is five years old and lame. And what that does to you, with the cruelty of not fitting in and the taunts and unable to care for himself, we can only guess. But it twisted his self-image.

In fact, Mephibosheth's original name was a Hebrew name meaning "Contender with Baal." But Mephibosheth changed his name; Mephiboseth means "man of shame." And he gave that name to himself. What is the name that you have given to yourself, the name that is so shameful and secretive that you've never told anyone? That's who you think you are. That is your identity to yourself.

Mephibosheth never felt like he belonged in David's palace. Why did he feel that way? It was from that tragic accident that originated back in his childhood; *something that he wasn't even responsible for*; something that was done to him. Listen to what the Spirit is speaking to you in your heart. There are things that happen to us in our childhood, and we have let them define us. There are things that happened to you that you were not even responsible for but that keep you, right now, from being able to see yourself as a son to God in whom He is well-pleased, a man or woman deserving of the inheritance. You see yourself as the estranged friend in Jesus' parable.

People grow up in alcoholic homes or abusive homes or as the odd one out and never fit and never belong. Some people were sexually abused or physically abused, or even grew up under the heavy weight of a legalism that you could never aspire to and you were never good enough. You carry that (all of shame, all of that unworthiness) with you into this relationship with your Papa God, and you just can't see yourself as the one deserving, the one who is the son in whom Papa is well-pleased. All you see is your unworthiness from things that happened in your life that were not even your fault.

You say, "Pastor, you don't know; there are things I've done that are so bad." Listen to me, *we were born broken*. Do you get that? You had a sin nature that you inherited. It was not your fault. And even though we acted out of that and took ownership of that by acting out, God knows you in that weakness. He knows what you had to face as a human, and He is not holding you accountable for it. He put it on Jesus. Jesus took it all; He bought your failures from you. You don't owe a thing.

You are not Mephibosheth, man of shame, any longer. You are not the estranged friend banging on the shut doors of heaven. How does God see you? God has given you a new name. Son! Son! So stop judging yourself by the law and by failure; that is the broad and wide way to destruction that many people go down. The Holy Spirit is bathing you in love. Love and grace are the only things that heal those deep wounds. He wants to heal you because He wants you to begin to see yourself as the wealthiest person in the land, mightily blessed, perfectly righteous, partaker of the inheritance because that's who you are. *Ask. Just ask!!* That is the New Covenant. You are curled up in bed with Papa. You are His family. He loves being with you. You are not a pauper. You are not a beggar. You are not an inconvenience. You need to see yourself as God sees you. You need to see your loving Papa as He is. The Sermon on the Mount is not an interesting theology; *it is the power of a new reality.*

THE SERMON ON THE MOUNT

Part 4 — IDENTIFYING FALSE PROPHETS

The whole Sermon on the Mount is these two ideas that Jesus is introducing: you have the Law Covenant way to God that Jesus says is the wide and broad way to destruction that everyone takes. It is the common way — do good, work hard, try to get God to bless you, and try to be good enough to get to heaven. That is the broad way that leads to destruction. And then you have the narrow, crowded out way that leads to eternal life. It is narrow because it is Christ alone and *"there is no other name under heaven given among men by which we must be saved"* (Acts 4). So it is narrow *and* it is crowded out. The KJV says it's a difficult way (narrow and difficult), but that is not a good translation of the word. Young's Literal Translation says "the way *is narrow and compressed*; it is crowded out by the prevailing voices of religious people that say you must work to earn God's favor."

So now we have these two ways that Jesus has spelled out: the way of receiving God's own righteousness as a gift that He gives to you (through Jesus) just by you asking, and the way of working hard and toiling and trying to maintain your own righteousness which leads to destruction. Jesus says this: *"Beware of false prophets, who come to you in sheep's clothing, but inwardly they are ravenous wolves. You will know them by their fruits. Do men gather grapes from thorn bushes or figs from thistles? Even so, every good tree bears good fruit, but a bad tree bears bad fruit. A good tree cannot bear bad fruit, nor can a bad tree bear good fruit. Every tree that does not bear good fruit is cut down and thrown into the fire. Therefore by their fruits you will know them"* (Matthew 7:15-20).

This was always a condemning passage when I was a Christian Pharisee, but I tried to not think about it too much. In my mind, if I thought about it too much, it would bring condemnation on me. I would think, "Am I a good tree or a bad tree?" And then I would think, "Well, sometimes I produce bad fruit, if I'm honest. Sometimes I produce good fruit, too (I do good things) but sometimes I produce bad fruit (I do bad things). Let's just not go there. Because if you produce bad fruit, you must be a bad tree and if you are a bad tree then you get thrown into the fire. But maybe if I get my bad fruit under the blood of Jesus (every time I produce it), then I get another chance at just producing good fruit, the slate is cleaned, and I get to start over." But I would wonder if I was a bad tree.

The kicker was in verse 18, *"A good tree cannot bear bad fruit."* It cannot! Nor can a bad tree bear good fruit. It cannot. So, here is how we think; "Jesus just said a good tree is incapable of producing bad fruit. I produce bad fruit; therefore, there is only one conclusion — I am a bad tree." If that is something you have wondered about, then this teaching is going to set you free. You are not a bad tree; no one in Christ is a bad tree.

This is why you need to understand the Sermon on the Mount because you cannot jump into the middle of it, take a scripture like this out of context, and expect to understand it. Jesus has been given a flowing argument that just "crescendos" with the new paradigm of God as your Papa. You are inside the house with Him, He loves you, you ask for His righteousness, He gives it as a gift, you ask for anything else you need, and He gives it because it's your inheritance. That is the new paradigm. But to embrace the new paradigm Jesus has to help them give up on and leave the law system of relating to God.

He has introduced the grace system in the middle of Chapter 7, and then He says, *"Beware of false prophets"* (verse 15). He is not talking about the average Joe believer trying to understand Him. He is warning them against listening to false prophets. False prophets are going to be those who look harmless (they are dressed as sheep), but they are teaching the wide and broad way that leads to destruction. They are not teaching the word of Jesus, the word full of Grace and Truth; they are teaching the list of rules to get right and stay right with God by your effort.

What makes it more confusing is that they look harmless, they look like sheep, they look like us; and (get this) they even use the name of Jesus, so they talk some of the talk. Look at verses 21-23: *"Not everyone who says to me, 'Lord, Lord,' shall enter the kingdom of heaven* (this is a continuation of the false prophets section; this is what happens to *false prophets*) *but he who does the will of my Father in heaven. Many will say to me in that day, 'Lord, Lord, have we not prophesied in your name* (this is amazing, they are using Jesus name!), *cast out demons in your name, and done many wonders in your name?'"* Each thing that they do is done in the name of Jesus. They think that they are doing the Father's will and they are ministering in Jesus' name, but they are *not* doing the Father's will.

Jesus says in verse 23, *"And then I will declare to them, 'I never knew you; depart from me, you who practice lawlessness!'"* Yikes! These are the people doing ministry. These are the false prophets. They are doing good things! They are doing many wonders, casting out demons, prophesying in Jesus' name. They are convinced that they are doing the will of the Father. And they are completely deluded. They are leading people (and have led themselves) down the wide and broad path to destruction. They are not leading people into the righteousness of God, God's own righteousness as a gift. And because they are not leading them to the only righteousness that a human can attain to, *they are practicing lawlessness* (the exact opposite of what they *think* they are doing).

They missed the will of the Father. What is the will of the Father? It's not in doing. It's in believing! *"Then they said to Him, 'What shall we do that we may work the works of God?' Jesus answered and said to them, 'This is the work of God, that you believe in Him whom He sent'"* (John 6:28-29). Believe in Jesus. Believe in the New Covenant that He provides. Believe in the Word of God full of *grace* and *truth!* Believe in the covenant full of grace, filled up with grace.

The false prophets, even though they use the name of Jesus and even though miracle things happen when His name is used, are not setting people free into grace, into simple belief in the beautiful name of Jesus. They are keeping people in bondage to the old way, the broad way, the wide way that leads to destruction. They look like us, they say "Jesus" things, they do religious works, but Jesus says they are ravenous wolves. Think about that expression "ravenous wolves." A wolf is a fierce predator. In our society we are not in touch with how dangerous a wolf can be. There was a news story recently about a Russian lady out in the sticks of Russia who was attacked by a wolf and fended it off, and actually killed it with a small hatchet. She was an elderly Russian lady and the nation lifted her up as a hero because wolves are so dangerous.

Jesus knew the Tanach (what we call the Old Testament scriptures). He knew the Word of God. He quoted it against the devil, taught from it, and after His resurrection when He met the two on the road to Emmaus it says that *"beginning at Moses and all the prophets, He expounded to them in all the scriptures the things concerning Himself."* Now, knowing that, Jesus calls the false prophets "ravenous wolves." There is only *one other time* in all of Scripture that expression is used. In Genesis 49:27: *"Benjamin is a ravenous wolf; in the morning he shall devour the prey, and at night he shall divide the spoil."* This is the prophecy that Jacob gave over each of his sons, each son who would together become the twelve tribes of Israel. And he called Benjamin a "ravenous wolf."

You have to know that from Benjamin and from another son, from Judah, would come the two great kings of God's people. Those two kings represent the two covenants of God; Saul, the first king who represents the Law Covenant (the rule of law). Saul comes out of Benjamin. God did not want Saul for His people, but the people insisted on it. This is the Old Covenant of law. God did not want the Law Covenant for His people, but the people insisted on it rather than intimacy and grace. *"Everything you have commanded us, Lord, we will do."* In other words, "We will relate to you based on this law." And Saul became a burden to the people as king. Even while he reigned, God anointed another king to take his place — David, from the tribe of Judah. David represents the New Covenant of grace in Jesus (the lion of the tribe of Judah).

Everything in the Old Testament is given as a picture for us to see Jesus. When Saul died and David became king, not a single one of the other tribes would recognize his kingship. All the other tribes sided with the descendant of Saul. That was the Jewish response to Jesus. Jesus came, the Jews rejected him. David came and the Jews rejected him until they came to the end of the law. When Isbosheth, the son of Saul, died, then they recognized David as king. I believe that this is a prophetic picture. One day, the Jews will recognize their king: King Jesus.

Saul was from the tribe of Benjamin that represented the Law of God in typology in Israel's history. And Benjamin here, representing the law, is called a "ravenous wolf." The tribe that represents the Law Covenant in Saul is a ravenous wolf. Not a single other time is that mentioned in the Bible — *until Jesus*. And Jesus says to beware of the false prophets, the ones who lead you down the wide, broad way of your own righteousness (the way of the law); they are ravenous wolves. They are descendants of Saul, descendants of the Law Covenant. And even though they have evolved a little bit, even though they wear sheep wool on the outside, they will kill you and they will lead you to destruction.

Some prophets want to feed the sheep. Others want to *feed on* the sheep. Some give them food. Some *make them* food. False prophets make you feel chewed up, chewed on. Some prophets give you a full belly and you leave feeling good. Some slash and tear at you — you leave feeling like you are never good enough for God and that reinforces the wall between you and your heavenly Father. What kind of prophet are you listening too?

Jesus said, *"You will know them by their fruit."* A good tree produces good fruit. A bad tree produces bad fruit. Now what does this mean? Jesus tells us. Look at verse 16: *"Do men gather grapes from thorn bushes or figs from thistles?"* He is looking at this from the hearer's perspective. The fruit He is talking about is not the personal works of good or bad works that the prophet is bearing in his life. Men don't gather your personal good works to feed on them. This is not good works — bad works. This is not, "Oh, your pastor had a beer at the local restaurant; look at that bad fruit." My point is that this is not talking about personal fruit of holy living versus unholy living. Jesus said, *"Do men gather grapes from thorn bushes or figs from thistles?"* The fruit of the prophet, in this little parable, is what the people collect in order to eat it. Do men gather grapes from thorn bushes? What are men doing? They are gathering fruit from prophets in order to eat the fruit.

Jesus is clearly talking about the words that the prophets are speaking. You will know the ravenous wolves by their words, which are their fruit. What kind of fruit do they produce? What do thorn bushes and thistles produce? The only thing thorn bushes and thistles produce are more thorn bushes and thistles.

In the Seed and Sower parables, Jesus called the thorns "worries and anxieties of this world." The fears of this world choke the good seed so that it becomes unfruitful. Jesus explains it plainly in that parable and He uses it again here. Jesus is clearly referring back (again) to the only place in the rest of the entire Bible where thorns and thistles are used: Genesis 3:17.

This is right after the fall of Adam and Eve, and they were thinking (in the Garden) that they must do something to improve themselves in order to be like God. That is the sin of Adam and Eve. The serpent gets them to believe a lie, that they are *not* created in God's image already, that they must *do* something. So they eat of the tree of the knowledge of good and evil, and they begin relating to God based on their knowledge of their own good works and bad works. Thousands of years later, Jesus is trying to deliver the world from that evil system — the wide broad way to destruction.

And God says to them (of the way that they have chosen) *"Cursed is the ground for your sake, in toil you shall eat of it all the days of your life, both thorns and thistles it shall bring forth from you"* (Genesis 3:17).

The fears and anxieties (Jesus said) just come up out of this world and can choke the good seed of grace. And then here in this parable, Jesus said that you have false prophets, who are thorn and thistle producers. Men go to gather fruit from them — good fruit from them — but all you can get from someone who is under the law system is thorns and thistles, worries and fears.

And friends, that is the only thing that the law system is capable of producing. If you are relating to God based on the tree of the knowledge of good and evil, if you are relating to God based on your efforts at doing right and doing wrong, you will *never* find peace, you will never find rest for your soul, and you will always be in fear of God, whether you are under His wrath or whether He is going to teach you a lesson through cancer or sickness or some such other nonsense. I don't care how many times a preacher uses the word "Jesus." If they don't understand that Jesus has made one sacrifice for all sin for all time and sat down so that the work of forgiveness of sins is done, and if they don't understand that God *"was in Christ reconciling the world to Himself not counting their sins against them"* (2 Corinthians 5:19), then they will be incapable of feeding the grapes, the wine of the new covenant, to God's people. The people will always be in fear because all this prophet has to give them is the curse of the law; the fears, the thorns and thistles that result from our own unrighteousness before God.

A bad tree *cannot* produce the good fruit of the New Covenant in people. That kind of prophet will give you a little Jesus, and then they will tell you that you better get right with God. A preacher of the law would *never* allow themselves to speak the pure word of grace, the word of God's righteousness as a pure gift of grace to poor in spirit people, unworthy people. Their conscience would not allow them to do that.

Look at this verse 17: *"A bad tree bears bad fruit."* Now the English translation uses the word "bad" two times here. A bad tree produces bad fruit. Jesus did not say it exactly that way. He uses two different adjectives. He says in the Greek that a *"poneros"* tree bears *"sapron"* fruit. The definition of the word *"poneros"* from Thayer's Greek Lexicon, says "full of labors, annoyances, hardships, pressed and harassed by labors, bringing toils." That is *"poneros."* That is Jesus' description of the kind of tree we're dealing with here. The false prophet tree, the very nature of this kind of tree is a *poneros* tree — full of labors, full of toiling. That is the Old Covenant. That is the system of Satan, the system that he introduced, the system that brought the curse. That kind of tree, a *poneros* tree, will only bear *sapron* fruit. *"Sapron"* means "rotten, putrid." In allegory it means morally worthless. The law does not produce righteousness. Just the opposite, it keeps people in bondage to their unrighteousness. The *poneros* (toiling to please God) tree only produces rotten fruit. It keeps people in uncomfortable fear, and reminds them of their sin. It does not free them. It keeps them in their putridness and in their rottenness.

God wants to free us with the only thing that can free us: the Gospel of Jesus, righteousness as a gift of grace. You are righteous because of Jesus. He took all of your unrighteousness — all of it. He took that with Him on the cross and He set you free from all your sin debt and gave to you His righteousness. His righteousness doesn't come on you sometimes and leave at other times. It is given in Jesus, and it remains on you just as He promised to never leave you or forsake you. You are never forsaken to your unrighteousness again. When you do unrighteous things, you still remain (in reality, in truth) the righteousness of God in Christ. Now that will strengthen you towards God and give you peace and joy.

False prophets can't produce that. False prophets make people eat thistles and thorns. They make people afraid. Jesus says to you *"Do not be afraid."* False prophets want you to fear your Father. False prophets are like fathers who pass out stones and serpents to eat. Stones are the law of God written on stone; the serpent is the system of the devil that was introduced in the garden and in which the whole world believes.

That's the wrong message. God is your Papa, who gives to His kids the gift of righteousness just by them asking. What does He give? He gives His kids bread! He gives His kids the bread of life, Jesus, as a gift. And He makes the declaration over His people, "I remember your iniquities no more. You are now my sons." Sons do not strive to be sons. They just are. Papa says, "Just enjoy being in the family with me again."

Just like a *poneros* tree cannot produce the good fruit of the kingdom of grace, a good tree (a prophet who finally gets the word of grace) cannot and will not preach law ever again. They will only preach the good news of Jesus. I would sincerely rather die than ever go back to mixing law and grace, mixing the two covenants. I just could not do it. A good tree cannot produce bad fruit. A bad tree only knows how to produce fear in people to keep them toiling and working to stay right with God. You will know them by their fruit. Don't eat that fruit of fear.

We know Papa. We know He is love. And His perfect love for you casts out fear. That's how you know you are listening to the real deal or not. Is it casting out fear? Is Jesus saying to you by the prophet, "Do not be afraid?" Is Jesus raising you up on your feet again? Is Jesus reminding you of your righteousness? Is He setting your heart to rest in Him? Is He telling you over and over again, "I have your life, start to finish, beginning to end, you are my *poiema*, my masterpiece (my workmanship)?" Is Jesus saying to you, "I made you qualified, I made you righteous, I made you whole, I perfected you forever, I have eternally redeemed you; come boldly to the throne of grace?" Jesus strengthens feeble knees. Listen to what He says about you! That is your identity. And "*by the abundance of grace and the gift of righteousness, you reign in life.*" That's you. Know who you are in Christ. Dismiss the false prophets. Spit out the thistles.

THE LORD'S PRAYER

Part 1 — OUR FATHER IN HEAVEN

"Our Father in heaven, hallowed be your name. Your kingdom come. Your will be done on earth as it is in heaven. Give us this day our daily bread. And forgive us our debts, as we forgive our debtors. And do not lead us into temptation, but deliver us from the evil one. For yours is the kingdom and the power and the glory forever. Amen. ("For if you forgive men their trespasses, your heavenly Father will also forgive you. But if you do not forgive men their trespasses, neither will your Father forgive your trespasses." — Matthew 6:9-13

I grew up learning three prayers by rote. The first prayer I learned is still precious to me (I learned it from my parents). I have an image in my mind's eye of my dad, bowing his head at the dinner table and all of us saying together, "God is great, God is good, let us thank Him for our food. Amen."

The second prayer I learned by rote was also taught to me by my folks. It was the "Now I lay me down to sleep" prayer. I hate that prayer. "If I should die before I wake, I pray the Lord my soul to take." Translation in my little kid mind: "God, if the boogey man under my bed comes out and kills me during the night; please, please, please don't send me to hell." I had a guilty conscience even then.

The third prayer I learned by rote was a prayer that my church taught me, the Lord's Prayer, which I memorized by virtue of the fact that we said it every week in worship. We were Presbyterians at that time, so we asked the Father to forgive us our *debts*, as we forgive our *debtors*. Presbyterians are wealthy people, so it made sense (in my child's mind) that we talked about money. In Pennsylvania where I grew up, it is fifty per cent Roman Catholic. I found out at Cub Scouts that Catholics asked God to forgive them their *trespasses*, and not *debts*. I found out later, as I was growing up, that it had nothing to do with trespassing on someone else's lawn or money, but that Jesus was talking about sins.

This is as close as it gets to Jesus instructing us to ask God for forgiveness for individual sins, except it's worse than that. Jesus ties our forgiveness to being able to forgive others. I've had many people come to me over the years who have had horrific things done to them when they were children (the absolute worst stuff you can imagine) and they are tormented because they know that deep down they still have unforgiveness toward their perpetrator. And because they have some residual unforgiveness, they wonder if they themselves are forgiven. That's what they think. Now where does that come from? It comes from this prayer — the Lord's Prayer.

I heard a popular Bible teacher on TV this last week. I won't say who, but you would all know him. He said in order to receive the blessing that God has for you, you have to do five things, and two of those things on the list were "send me money" and "root out any unforgiveness in your heart." He said if you have unforgiveness in your heart, you remain out of fellowship with God and God can't bless you. So he said to look inside and look for unforgiveness and once you get it out, *then* you will receive the blessing.

Now this is important business. If our forgiveness depends on this, we better get it right. Jesus taught His disciples to pray this way. But there's something that doesn't add up. Because the Apostle Paul, in all his epistles in the New Testament never tells the people that your forgiveness depends on your ability to forgive others. Nor do any of the other apostles; not Peter, not James, not John, not any of the recorded words of the apostles in the Book of Acts. They just say, *"Believe on the name of the Lord Jesus Christ and you will be saved." "Confess Jesus Christ, and you will be saved." "Believe in your heart, Jesus Christ, and you will be saved."*

So what's going on here? Is Jesus wrong? No, Jesus wasn't wrong — He was absolutely right. We were the ones who were wrong. We were wrong in teaching this prayer as a New Covenant prayer. We were wrong in teaching this prayer as a prayer that believers ought to model and pray. And I'm getting ready to slay a sacred cow here. But you and I need to face the fact that every now and then the church has interpreted some things wrongly through the years. Just because Jesus said it, doesn't mean it applies to New Covenant believers.

"How can you say that?" Because Jesus had two missions when He walked the earth: to bury the Jews under the law, and to introduce the New Covenant. It was to bury the Jews under the law, to show them that the law only condemns them (it does not help them). So Jesus said if you get angry at a person then you are under judgment. If you hate someone, you have already committed murder and will be judged accordingly by God. If your eye offends you, gouge it out; if your hand offends you, cut it off. Jesus was just as serious there as He is in the Lord's Prayer. There aren't too many TV preachers out there saying, "In order to receive your blessing: step one — cut off your hand if it sinned, and if you looked lustfully or in envy, gouge out your eye. Step two — send in your check or money order to . . .”

So Jesus was burying the Jews under the law to shut them up; the Bible says "to stop up their mouths" and get them to see that they needed a Savior. And then He came to introduce the New Covenant of grace, the covenant of total forgiveness in His name. The Book of Hebrews says that *"a covenant is enacted at the shedding of blood."* So when did the New Covenant in Jesus begin? At the shedding of His blood; His death. So when you read the gospels, you have to be (what Hebrews calls) *"skilled in the word of righteousness."* You have to be able to rightly divide the word of truth between Old Covenant and New Covenant because Jesus is the transitional figure.

Notice that this teaching that Jesus gave on the Lord's Prayer occurs at the very beginning of Jesus ministry. This is *the first* recorded teaching session that Jesus does — the Sermon on the Mount. So let me ask you, what covenant are the people under? They are under the Old Covenant, the Law Covenant. Under the Old Covenant of Law, you had to *do things* to get God to forgive you. You had to beg God to forgive you. You begged Him for forgiveness, you brought in an animal sacrifice, and that's the way you got your sin forgiven. But you could walk out of the temple clean and forgiven and then find the person who owes you, who harmed you, who sinned against you and get bitter at him (which Jesus says is the same as murder), and now you're back at square one all over again, needing forgiveness. Your state of forgiveness was dependent on how well you kept the law and how well you kept up with confessing, begging, and sacrificing. That was a bad deal. God found fault with that covenant. He knew it was faulty from the beginning, and that's why all along He had a better plan in store for us because He loves us.

There are believers who live like they are under the Old Covenant, thinking they have to confess sin to be forgiven. That is Anti-Christ. It is a direct assault on the work that Jesus did, which was one sacrifice for all sins for all time (Hebrews 10:9). If you don't believe that you were perfected forever when you asked Jesus to come into your life, you have missed the gospel. You have missed the very center of the New Covenant. You have missed the whole point of Jesus' sacrificial death on the cross. He came as the Lamb of God who has taken away the sins of the world — all of them — from the time of Adam, to the great and glorious Day of the Lord when He comes back again. Every sin is gone. Every sin is bought and paid for.

A friend of mine has conversations with a man who is Jewish and they were talking about this issue of forgiveness. On one occasion, the man said to my friend, "This is what I don't understand about you Christians; you say that Jesus paid the price for sins, but then the church says you have to confess your sins to be forgiven. It doesn't make sense. Which is it? Did Jesus take away the sins of the world, or didn't He?" He did. So what is this prayer about? This is Jesus teaching His disciples to pray to the Father within the boundaries of the covenant that they were then under — the Old Covenant. This is not a Christian's prayer. This is an Old Covenant prayer.

Nehemiah Gordon is a linguistic scholar and a Hebrew expert who is a Karaite Jew, a practicing Jew. He is not a believer, that's my point. This is what he says about the Lord's Prayer: "There is not a single word in this prayer that is contrary to the Jewish faith. Nothing in the prayer itself is contrary to Judaism. This is a Jewish prayer." Put those words in the framework of the two covenants; the covenant of law or the covenant of grace in Jesus. This is a Jewish, Old Covenant, Old Testament prayer.

Now there's one caveat to that — *Jesus begins to introduce a new intimacy with Yahweh God.* All through the Sermon on the Mount, He has been calling God "Father," and He applies that here in this prayer. Call God "Father." Pray, *"Our Father in Heaven."* In the Hebrew, the word for father is just two letters: Aleph, Beth (*"av"*). When St. Paul says that we have been given the Spirit of Christ whereby we cry out, "Abba, Father," he is adding another aleph to the end of the word "daddy" and what that does is make it definitive. It's like saying, "You're not just a father, not just a daddy to me; you are *the* daddy, my one and only daddy, my one and only Papa." The Holy Spirit grows you to a place where you say, "Papa God, you are my one and only Father, my one and only Papa Father." Isn't that what the Spirit is teaching you to say? He's teaching me to say that.

I have heard preachers say (and I've probably said it myself) that nowhere in the Old Testament is God referred to as Father and what Jesus is doing is revolutionary in this prayer. Okay, what Jesus is doing *is* revolutionary in this prayer; in fact, I believe that what Jesus is doing is pointing directly to the New Covenant in calling God "Father." And the reason I believe that is because the idea of God as a Father *is* in the Old Testament, but it is a prophetic scripture about the Messiah. This is God talking to King David — *"When your days are fulfilled and you rest with your fathers, I will set up your seed after you who will come from your body, and I will establish His kingdom. He shall build a house for my name, and I will establish the throne of His kingdom forever. I will be His Father, and He shall be my son"* (2 Samuel 7:12-14).

Jesus takes that truth and says, "I am the Son whose kingdom is being established forever. He's my Father. And guess what, I invite you into this same relationship. You get to call Him Father too." This is a hint of the New Covenant that was soon going to be instituted. Jesus is essentially saying, "things are getting ready to change around here and here's how it will be: I am the Son, Yahweh is Father, I am in Him, He is in me, and one day soon, you will be in me. And if you are in me and I am in the Father, then you are in the Father, just like the Son." That is part of Jesus' high priestly prayer in John 15. "But for now, just start practicing. God is not in you, but He is still your Father."

Notice that Jesus teaches them to pray, *"Our Father in heaven."* That's Old Covenant. That's pre-Holy Spirit, before the outpouring of the Holy Spirit at Pentecost. Not understanding that this is an Old Covenant prayer messes people up. Our Father *in heaven*. Where is God? Oh, God is out there. Like, way out there, and your prayers have to ascend to heaven.

I can't tell you how many times people have told me, "Pastor, it just seems like my prayers don't make it past the ceiling. It's like my prayers just bounce back to me, like they don't make it to heaven." Listen, if you were still under the Old Covenant and the Old Covenant way of praying to your Father in heaven, you might be right to worry about that. But God is no longer just the Father in heaven; *He's the Abba in you!* The reason you bow your head when you pray is because you're talking to God who is right here inside you!

In the New Covenant, your body is the Temple of God, the place where He chooses to dwell. Abba is in you. *"Do you not know that your body is the temple of His Spirit?"* That means you could whisper and He

53

hears it. That means that you could just think it, and He thinks it with you. And the beauty of it is that He likes being there. He loves being in you. Papa God is also in a real place called Heaven; that's part of what makes Him God. But if you're relating to God as the one who is out there, somewhere in heaven, you are not relating to Him based on the New Covenant — you are relating to Him based on the Old Covenant. You are probably doing it because you were taught wrongly about *this prayer*.

If you feel like your prayers are not getting to the ears of God, your feelings are wrong. And if you think that God is out there in heaven when you pray, you need to change the way you think. *"Metaknoia!"* That word (that we translate as "repent") literally means "change the way you think." In the New Covenant we've got to get our heads around something new, and it is this: Jesus, by His sacrifice, made us fit places for Abba (Papa) to reside. And He likes being there, in you. *"He who raised Jesus from the dead* (that's the Father) *dwells in you"* (Romans 8:11). Papa in you. Not just the Spirit. Not just Jesus in me. Abba. Your one and only Father.

Jesus said, *"Our Father in heaven; hallowed be your name."* "Hallowed" is the word *"haggios,"* which means "holy." This is just the strangest verb tense with this word. In the Greek what they did was take an adjective (holy) and make a verb out of it. A literal translation goes something like this: "Let be being *holyized* the name of you." It is a command. It's the same tense that God uses in creation in Genesis 1:2 — "And God said, 'Let there be light.'" Literally, "light be." And Jesus is teaching Old Covenant people to speak out: "Let the name of God be *holyized*. God, let your name be made holy."

Isn't God's name holy already? This kind of begs the question — how do you make God's name holy? And what *is* God's name, anyway? God has a lot of titles. People talk about the names of God, but what they mean by the names of God are the "titles of God." God is *El-Shaddai* (God Almighty) but that's really not His name; that's a title. *Jehovah Tsidkenu* (the Lord is my righteousness) strictly speaking, is not His name; that's His title.

If you ask a Jew what the name of God is, they will tell you straight out that it's not any of those. It is a name that God revealed to Moses, the sacred name. His name is "Yahweh," best translated as "I AM." That's why the religious leaders were ready to stone Jesus to death for blasphemy when He said, *"Before Abraham was, I AM."* Look at this from John 8:58-59: *"Jesus said to them, "Most assuredly, I say to you, before Abraham was, I AM." Then they took up stones to throw at Him."* Why were they so mad? Because He put Himself in the place of God.

I don't know if you noticed before or not, but right after that, Jesus uses this whole string of "I AM" teachings. He puts Himself in the place of God in John 8. Then, just to make sure you get it, *"I am the light of the world"* (John 9). *"I am the door"* (John 10:7). *"I am the good Shepherd"* (I thought The Lord was my Shepherd, I AM is my shepherd; Yes, I AM that Shepherd) (John 10:14). *"I am the resurrection and the life"* (John 11:28). *"I am the way the truth and the life"* (John 14:6). *"I am the vine"* (John 15:1). God's name is "I AM," and "I AM that I AM." "I am the name of God," says Jesus.

The name of God is defined in two places: in Moses as Yahweh (I AM), and then once in the New Testament where God tells you who He is. "And she will bring forth a son, and you shall call His name,

Jesus, for He will save His people from their sins" (Matthew 1:21). The Greek name Jesus (*"iehsus"*) doesn't mean anything. The name Jesus in English doesn't mean anything. God revealed Himself in Jesus; He said who "I AM" is when He revealed His name to Joseph and Mary. He is "Yeshua." Yeshua is the shortened form of the Hebrew name "Yehoshua" which means "Yahweh saves" or "the Lord saves." "Yahweh saves" is just gibberish. Translate it out. Yahweh means "I AM." Yehoshua means "I AM saves." *The one we call Jesus, was Papa God revealed (the express image of the Father) in the flesh; "I AM" in the flesh who has come to save.*

Jesus is the rest of the name of God. When Jesus taught them to pray *"Hallowed be thy name,"* He was teaching the Jews to pray a prayer that got them ready to accept the full name of God. What is the full name of God? *"I AM saves you. I AM rescues you."* How does He rescue you? Go back to what the angel said about the completed name of God. *"You shall call His name Yehoshua* (I AM saves) *for* (because) *He will save His people from their sins"* (Matthew 1:21). Jesus is getting His listeners ready to receive Him as the one who will forgive all their sins!

When you pray for something to be holy, you are praying that it be set apart for God's use. That's the definition of holy. A pulpit that is set aside entirely for God's use would be considered a holy pulpit. When you pray that the full name of God be holy, you're praying that it be set apart entirely for God's use, that it be seen as holy (in other words "as from God"), and that it be received as holy (the use to which God intended it). You can only pray that prayer and make that so *for yourself.* You have no power to *holyize* the name of God except to yourself. You can tell people, "You should hallow God's full name," but that does not hallow it to them. They may quit using Yehoshua as a swear word but even if they quit saying it that way, it doesn't mean inward transformation has occurred.

This is a prayer that Jesus taught them to pray for themselves. "Let the full name of God be seen and received in all of its power and to the full extent that God has for it." What Jesus was teaching them to pray, through the back door, was that they would be ready to receive Him when the time came for the revealing of the Son of God.

"I AM saves you from your sins." This is Jesus' nod to a New Covenant, a new way of finding forgiveness. Who saves you from your sins? Not you. Not your confession of them, not your sacrifices for them, not you begging God for mercy. God takes forgiveness out of your hands and He reveals His full name. "I AM saves you." You aren't saving you. I AM saves you. When you receive Jesus for who He is, the Lamb of God who has taken away all of the sins of the entire world forever by His one sacrifice, you have hallowed the full name of God. And if you can't get your head around that, then the name of Jesus is not holy unto you; it's common, like any other name. The opposite of holy (set apart) is not unrighteous. The opposite of holy is common. If Jesus hasn't taken away all sin, you make it less holy. You make it more common. You make it unholy. Just receive Him for who He is. Your sins are gone. Get over it. Even the ones you do today. Abba has made His home in you. And He likes it. He loves it. Now that's some good news!

THE LORD'S PRAYER

Part 2 — THY KINGDOM COME

"Our Father in heaven, hallowed be your name. Your kingdom come. Your will be done." —Matthew 6:9-10

Just think about *"your kingdom come"* — just that. Why was Jesus teaching the people to pray this? That's the right question to ask. The wrong question to ask is, "What does this mean for us?" Because the church is always jumping to "what does this mean for us" before it even understands the context.

I've heard this wrongly preached as a call for Jesus to come back. "Jesus, come on back and establish your thousand year reign. Let's get evil vanquished forever at your coming, and let's establish righteousness on the earth, let your glory be revealed. Let your kingdom finally come." That's what everyone wanted in Jesus' day. Frankly, that's what we want too. "Come, Lord Jesus." If He came back this afternoon, how awesome would that be! I'd be stoked. The thing is — that is not what Jesus is teaching people to pray. He's not teaching people to pray for the earthly, physical kingdom of the Messiah to be set up on earth. Everyone wanted that in Jesus' day. Throw off the shackles of Roman tyranny, Messiah is set up to rule, the Jews will be in charge. Everyone wanted that with Jesus. But Jesus knew it wasn't time for that. The kingdom doesn't start there. It doesn't start on the outside; it doesn't start externally like an army coming in from the outside and occupying a territory. That's not the way God has set this up to happen. *It starts on the inside.*

Jesus was making this clear to His hearers. This prayer was taught in the midst of the Sermon on the Mount. Just look at how Jesus was getting the people to think about the kingdom of God in the Sermon on the Mount. In fact, the very first word out of Jesus' mouth (in the Sermon on the Mount) is Kingdom teaching. "Blessed are the poor in spirit, for theirs is the kingdom of heaven."

The kingdom, the benefits of the kingdom, being part of the kingdom, is linked with something going on inside of a person. It's not whether they *do* anything, as in "are you ready to take up a sword and defend my cause?" It's not, "are you ready to work really hard at being righteous?" It's not, "are you ready to pray hard, do evangelism, and keep the law of God with all your strength?" *No, the kingdom belongs to people who have given up.* The kingdom belongs to the people who know that their efforts at righteousness stink. The kingdom belongs to the people who know that they are poor in spirit. That was *the* starting place for Jesus' ministry. He is turning their understanding of religion upside down. The first words in His public teaching are the starting place for receiving the kingdom.

Jesus is saying, "You can't be like the Pharisees, who think that in themselves (by their efforts), they are rich toward God. The kingdom doesn't belong to them. It can only belong to people who see their spiritual need; who admit their spiritual poverty. That is the starting place for coming into the kingdom." Is Jesus focusing them on the external or the internal? Is He focusing them on things you have to *do* to usher in the kingdom and be a part of it, or is He focusing them on your state of being, who you honestly are before God? It's your state of being. This is a different way to think for them.

The Law of God and the Ten Commandments are a picture of what the kingdom of God looks like when it comes to us from the outside in. That way doesn't work. How does it look when it comes from the outside in (in the form of God's law)? It looks like failure. It looks like increased sin. Is the law sin? "No," Paul says, "God forbid!" But when the kingdom of God is external and comes to us from the outside in, it's disastrous. If God just chose to come back and impose His kingdom on humanity (from the outside) we would all be goners. Evil would be dealt with apart from Jesus. And no one would be left standing.

In this prayer, Jesus wasn't teaching the people to pray, "Come and get them, God; your kingdom come. Just bring it on. Just impose your righteousness from the outside in." That's what the Pharisees wanted. But we would all be sunk if He did that, Pharisees included. What we have to remember is that "God so loved the world." That's why Jesus came. God is not up there going, "Oh, I want to just be done with the human problem in the universe. Just pray, 'Oh come God, your kingdom come. Just finish with this humanity problem.'" No, He loves humans. He loves you. He became one of us to save us. How? *From the inside out.*

The kingdom of God begins inside of a person. *"Now when He was asked by the Pharisees when the kingdom of God would come, He answered them and said, "The kingdom of God does not come with observation nor will they say, 'See here!' or 'See there!' For indeed, the kingdom of God is within you"* (Luke 17:20-21). What does that mean? It means it is not external, it is internal. It means that it is not what you do — it is who you are. It is being, not doing.

"The kingdom of God is not eating and drinking" (Romans 14:17). What is that? External stuff. And Paul

was talking about keeping the law of God. He was talking here about doing righteous things. The kingdom of God is not about cleaning up your act and doing the right thing, doing works of righteousness to get in good with God, *"but righteousness and peace and joy in the Holy Spirit."* Now listen, that's a flow. That's an internal progression. You accept the righteousness of God that He gives to you as a gift. When you finally get your head around that and when you finally get your head around the fact that He has perfected your spirit forever, that you are the "righteousness of God in Christ Jesus," truly righteous in your spirit forever, then what flows out of that? Peace, peace before God. I mean, no more striving. No more wondering if God is pleased with you. No more wondering if you've been good enough. Just resting in his righteousness. Peace. Relaxing before God. Peace flows out of righteousness. And when you get the fact of your own righteousness and you enter into peace and rest, what flows out of that? Joy! Joy! So much joy you have to express it.

Recently I was just receiving the goodness of the Lord, and I got to place where I just shouted out! No one was in the house and the neighbors may have thought I was crazy, but I shouted out, "God! You are so good! I love you!" There's a place and time for everything, isn't there? That's worship. People who finally get righteousness, also get real peace, and from that peace flows joy! I am happier now than I have ever been in my entire life. It's not an act. I don't conjure it up. I have problems like everyone else, but when I get my mind on Jesus and who I am in Christ and how righteous I am, I just find peace. And when I am in peace, I just find happiness.

Paul says *that* is the kingdom of God. That is the kingdom getting dominance in you. That is exactly what Jesus was talking about — "your kingdom come." Where? *In me.* I mentioned the first verse of the Sermon on the Mount, but the very next time Jesus mentions the kingdom it is connected to righteousness. *"Blessed are those who are persecuted for righteousness' sake, for theirs is the kingdom of heaven"* (Matthew 5:10). Jesus knew that the people who accepted His gift of righteousness would be persecuted. Strangely, they are not persecuted by the unbelieving world, but by God's people. This is one of the identifiers of believers, for those who possess the kingdom — they are persecuted for the righteousness Jesus gave them. "Well, you can't just rest in what Jesus did. You need to stay away from sin and nip it in the bud. Nip it in the bud!" Well, sure, but my righteousness does not depend on that. Religious people hate this message.

I got a nasty email recently, just toxic. Why? Because I won't back down on this message and where it is leading us. I just bless them and send it back with a blessing. So the kingdom of God starts internally and flows out. The Greek word for kingdom is *"basilleia."* *Basilleia* isn't a reference to external stuff like castles or armies; it literally means "the reign or the rule, or the power displayed of a certain entity." So when you talk about the kingdom of God, you are talking about the reign and rule of God, His very power unleashed inside of a person.

Jesus said, "Pray to the Father, 'your kingdom come.'" He was teaching the people to pray for the reign and rule of God to come. How? Inside of them — that God's power (His purpose, what He says, what He thinks, what He's doing) would be unleashed internally in a person. That was going to begin at Pentecost, at the giving of the Holy Spirit. The Holy Spirit is God's presence and power unleashed inside of a person.

Up until this time, the kingdom of God had only been unleashed inside of Jesus. It happened at His baptism. This is from Mark 1:10-11: *"And immediately, coming up from the water, He saw the heavens parting and the Spirit descending upon Him like a dove. Then a voice came from heaven, 'You are my beloved Son, in whom I am well pleased.'"* So the Holy Spirit comes to Jesus. Jesus limited himself. He was God, and yet He limited Himself as a man. He let go of His godly right, emptied Himself, and became like us. And when He received the Holy Spirit, He received Him just like you receive Him. When the Father spoke to Jesus from heaven, He spoke to Him the same words that He speaks to you when you allow the reign and rule of God (His presence) to come into you. The moment you received Him, before you had a chance to do anything for Him, the Father said to you, "You are my beloved son, in whom I am well pleased."

God is well pleased with you the moment He dwells in you; apart from anything you do, apart from good works, apart from coming to church, apart from all the things you do, good or bad. When He came into you, He made you good and called you "son." And Jesus was teaching His people to pray for the time when this coming of the kingdom would be revealed to people. That has happened. The prayer was answered. They prayed, "Thy kingdom come." God said, "Yes!" It has come perfectly inside of everyone who receives Jesus. And it's up to you to believe that God brought the kingdom to you. God's kingly rule has been brought to you. The proof is in the pudding. Everything is changed. You begin walking by the power and leading of the Holy Spirit.

I know a pastor who likes to say that grace changes three things: the way you see God, the way you see yourself, and the way you see others. *That is the fulfillment of the law.* What is the greatest commandment? "Love the Lord your God with everything in you. And the second is like unto it, you shall love your neighbor as yourself." Jesus said that the entire law and the prophets are summed up in that. Except that's not really two commandments — it's three. It is "love God, love your neighbor, and love yourself." Before the kingdom of God was revealed to me, I strove to love God (but most of the time I was mad at Him and disappointed in Him and afraid of Him). I strove to love other people (but it was mostly a show to make myself feel better), and I hated myself. I loathed myself for my failings.

The New Covenant (the kingdom of God coming to you!) causes you to love God (for what He's done — you just can't help it) and, miraculously, I think, causes you to love yourself. And this is the truth; this is just a psychological fact, you can't love other people until you love yourself. Your love of others, in the end, will reflect how much you love yourself.

This is why so many marriages are absolutely dreadful, because everyone can start out doing nice things for people who pay attention to them. But in the end, you will reflect back to your spouse the view that you have of yourself. If you see yourself as never measuring up, as always falling short of the mark and you are hard on yourself for not being the person you want to be, guess what, you will inevitably start judging your spouse the same way. They can never do enough and what they do will never be good enough, and no amount of doing will please them. If you belittle yourself, you will belittle your spouse. If you don't have self-love, you will be self-centered. You will be trying to get from your spouse what only God and His view of you can give you.

Some people think that love of self is actually sinful, but I have learned that love of yourself, seeing yourself the way God sees you ("You are my beloved son in whom I am well pleased") is part of the divine and eternal triangle of love that will be in place forever and ever. That is God's love for you, yours for Him, and your love for yourself. And flowing from that is your love for others. In my experience of life, I found no love for myself until I actually started believing God's view and opinion of me.

I went to a Women Aglow meeting many years ago at the beginning of my ministry, and I was the guest speaker. A woman from my church, a godly, spirit-filled woman, got up to introduce me in front of the one hundred or so women there. She said, "God gave me this word for Pastor Greg, as the way to introduce him." She said to the crowd, "Don't take this as blasphemy, but God gave me this word: 'This is my beloved Son, in whom I am well pleased.'"

Man, my heart just sank in my spirit because I knew that that was not true. But how wrong I was! God tried to teach me this from the very start of my ministry! It is true! This is God's view of you. And you must accept it. This is the kingdom of God come into you. It changes everything.

Take it from someone who wasted twenty years of ministry, twenty years of my adult life. I guarantee you this is God saying this to you: "You are my beloved son, and I am so pleased with you." He is so pleased with you. Not for anything you've done or not done, but because you simply have faith in His Son. Jesus loved and valued you enough to die for you. You are valued! When you start getting your head around that, then you actually start believing that you may be a person of worth, a person of value, and you start loving yourself. And you fall in love with God because He first loved you. And then, from somewhere deep inside of you, this love works its way out of you to other people. And you start judging people less and seeing them (not as your enemy) but as broken people who just need more time to heal. And your heart actually goes out to them. You find yourself loving even your enemies. Why? Was it because Jesus said, "You must love your enemies?" No, it's because the kingdom of God has invaded your heart.

You want to tell people about God's love. And you want to reach out and bring healing to people. You actually come into your own, you come into the power God has for you to walk in, and you reach out to a person who is sick and pray the prayer of faith and take authority and you heal them. You do it. You heal them of cancer and you heal them of fibromyalgia. Why? Because the kingdom of God has come.

You want people freed from the bondage of condemnation; and so you give. I don't give my money to keep some institution going; I give because we're in the business of changing lives, transforming lives. This is the only thing that changes people — the kingdom coming to them. Not them earning the kingdom. *But the kingdom coming into them.* Hey, the kingdom is come! It is changing people from the inside out. It is a revolution. It blows me away, that I get to be a part of it. Hallelujah!

THE LORD'S PRAYER

Part 3 — GIVE US OUR DAILY BREAD

"In this manner, therefore, pray: Our Father in heaven, hallowed be your name. Your kingdom come. Your will be done on earth as it is in heaven. Give us this day our daily bread." — Matthew 6: 9-11

What is our daily bread? Anyone who has studied this prayer will quickly answer that your daily bread is the barest essentials needed for physical life. Bread here represents what you need today in the physical to get through the day. It represents food, it represents shelter, it represents money; in our culture it represents gasoline to get to work, clothing for the kids for school, strength in your body to do what needs done, all the essentials we need to live life.

Interestingly, most Christian prayer that I have heard through the years has been modeled after this petition. In other words, people are asking God for the bare essentials needed to live life. This makes sense to people. "God, I need some money to make this rent payment; God I need this, I need this." A lot of prayer is like that. It is asking God for the essentials of life and it is getting other people to stand in faith for you for the essentials of life. I'm not saying that all of that is wrong. There are times when our hearts are heavy for something that we feel needs to happen. By all means, you need to tell the Father about things that are bringing anxiety and things that are needful. That's relationship. But the point I want to make is that the

New Covenant in Jesus changed this petition. This is not a believer's request. I'll tell you why.

Asking God for daily bread, asking God for the essentials for living, assumes a closed heaven. It assumes a limited access to the kingdom of God. It assumes that there is a distant relationship between you and God and that He is requiring you to petition and ask for what you need before the hand of God will be open and your needs will be met. When you ask God for what you need, you are assuming His hand is presently closed to you. You are asking Him to open His hand. You are assuming that there is distance in the relationship, that He is not seeing what's going on with you, that something is out of whack that you have to fix in the relationship before you get what you need. That's what the people *before* the New Covenant in Jesus had to contend with. "Have I been good enough, have I done enough, have I made the right religious moves in order to get on God's good side so that He will take care of me?" That is exactly the Old Covenant.

Jesus at His death changed all that. He made the relationship right between you and God so that now you could call God "Father." The moment the New Covenant was enacted by Jesus at His death, things changed between humans and God. You were given the spirit by which you cry out "Abba Father," which means "My own Papa Daddy." We have got to get our heads around this.

I raised three kids. When my kids were little, my job as a parent was to see to their needs. Good parents are in tune with and anticipate the needs of their children. When I saw they needed new clothes, I didn't stand around and wait weeks for them to petition me and ask on their own for clothes and then get them one piece at a time. No, I got them clothes before they ever

68

asked, because I saw their need. When it was dinner time and they hadn't eaten for four hours, I knew that they were hungry. How sick would it have been for me to wait around and make them ask me for food before I fixed a meal for them? That is poor parenting, but people think that God is that way in His parenting. That is not the way it is with God under the New Covenant in Jesus.

Jesus gave the paradigm of the New Covenant just a few verses later in His Sermon on the Mount, and it is in stark contrast to this Old Covenant mode of praying where we petition God for what we need. Look at verse 31: *"Therefore do not worry, saying, 'What shall we eat?' or 'What shall we drink?' or 'What shall we wear?'"* This is in the context of relating to God. In other words, these are the prayers of people who don't know how things have changed. "God, what am I going to eat? Oh, God, what am I going to wear? How are my needs ever going to be met?" A lot of believers pray that way. Why? Because they don't believe they have a Papa Daddy. Look at verses 32-32: *"For after all these things the Gentiles seek. For your heavenly Father knows that you need all these things."* (He is a good parent; He knows your needs, He anticipates your needs.) How do your needs get filled? Here's the answer: *"But seek first the kingdom of God and His righteousness, and all these things shall be added to you."*

What is first on the agenda? The kingdom of God (That means the reign and rule and power of God unleashed inside of you) — His influence, His reign is a done deal that has been released inside of you. Seek to know that first "and His righteousness." Whose righteousness? His righteousness — not yours. Here's how a lot of people interpret this: "I have to do righteous things. I have to attain to His righteousness, and then I'll get what I need." No. You cannot attain to the righteousness of God. If that's what this means, then you will *never* get to that place and you will never get what you need from God. This is His righteousness, the righteousness, Paul says, that has been revealed apart from works, the gift of righteousness that God gives you and that cannot be taken away from you.

Paul says, "You have become the righteousness of God in Christ." It is a gift. You cannot mess this up. The Bible says you have been perfected forever! Not until the next time you sin. Hebrews 10 says that Jesus made one sacrifice for all sins, for all time (that means all of your sins — past sins, present sins, future sins) and He paid for them. Your sin problem is done away with. Nothing can now separate you from God and His love. Your sin does not separate you from God, ever, ever.

Jesus said if you understand kingdom power that is released inside of you and you understand that His righteousness as a gift is given to you, then you can *know* that your Papa Daddy is going to see to all your needs. You can have confidence in the *fact* that *"all these things are added to you."* Why? Because you are in fellowship with a good Papa. He is so good. Heaven is not closed to you who believe that.

Under the Old Covenant, it was closed. Heaven was closed, and you had to do things to open it. "If you keep the law, then you will receive blessing." And Isaiah the prophet longed for the time in the future when it would not be that way. And so he prophesied in Isaiah 64:1, *"Oh, that you would rend the heavens! That you would come down!"* Literally, "Oh God, that you would rip open the heavens." It was a longing for the blessing and power and revelation of heaven to no longer be closed up to people. This is the prophecy.

The fulfillment of the prophecy happened in Mark 1:10. This is the baptism of Jesus. *"And immediately, coming up from the water, He saw the heavens parting and the Spirit descending upon Him like a dove."* Literally, "He saw the heavens rent in two, and the Spirit descending upon Him." The prophecy of Isaiah was fulfilled on the day of Jesus' baptism. The heavens were ripped open, and the Spirit descended. *"Oh, that you would rend the heavens; that you would come down!"* The heavens were ripped open, and the Spirit descended. And there began a new era, a new way of living where we don't have to find some way to access the riches of heaven; but that in Jesus, heaven remains open to you. There is now, to you who believe, an open heaven. You live under an open heaven. The declaration of Jesus, the very first words out of His mouth when He began His ministry was, "The kingdom of heaven is at hand. It's right here. You can just reach out and partake. It is accessible to you."

If you believe that God made you righteous as a gift and nothing separates you (ever, ever) from His care and love and that you live under an open heaven and God is your attentive Papa Daddy, then you can know that what you need is provided, always. You don't seek daily bread; you possess more than you need. Everything has been added to you.

Because the Holy Spirit is so gentle and such a patient teacher, we are all learning how to pray. But today is a day when the Holy Spirit has brought you to a place of revelation. You need to accept it. Most of what passes itself off as Christian prayer is actually just asking God for things that you already have. Most Christians live in the ignorance of what they already possess and because of that, their prayers are unanswerable by God. For instance, (please take this the right way), out of concern for people, to show our love and compassion for people, we commonly pray, "Oh, God, please be with so-and-so." Well, under the New Covenant, the Spirit lives inside of us

71

permanently, and Jesus has promised to never leave us nor forsake us. So when you pray "Oh God, please be with so-and-so," you are praying a prayer that God cannot answer. Why? Because it is done already.

Jesus said that if you understand God's kingdom and His gift of righteousness, everything you need is now added to you. It belongs to you already. What else does it mean that we have received already every spiritual gift in the heavenlies (Ephesians 1:3)? Everything heaven has for you is already yours in Jesus. We need a new way to pray, and it isn't the Lord's Prayer. Instead of looking at the pattern that Jesus gave to people who were living under the Old Covenant, we need to see the example of Jesus Himself and how He prayed because He had the Father/Son relationship that is now the covenant relationship you have with God. So the way Jesus prayed is the way we ought to pray.

Let me lift up this observation to you: in all the recorded words of Jesus, He never asked the Father for daily bread. He never asked the Father to meet His needs (even when an overwhelming need presented itself). What did He do? How did He pray? He prayed like the need was already fulfilled and He thanked God instead of asking God.

Think about the feeding of the four thousand. Does Jesus ask the Father to "please feed these people who are hungry and who need to eat something?" Was Jesus trying to convince God of the need, trying to get the Father to see something that He hadn't seen so that God was up there going, "Oh, man, are you serious? They're all hungry? I didn't see that; thank you so much for cluing me in." Jesus knew that Papa Daddy saw the need. In fact, (think about this) it was Papa Daddy who gave Jesus the idea to feed them all. Jesus said, "I only do what I see the Father doing. I only say what I hear the Father say."

It was Papa Daddy who told Jesus, "Son, these people are hungry and I want to feed them before they go home." Jesus said, "I'm on it." So how did Jesus pray? *"And He took the seven loaves and the fish and gave thanks, broke them, and gave them to His disciples; and the disciples gave to the multitude"* (Matthew 15:10). He gave thanks. He thanked God in advance for what God was about to do. Now you cannot truly thank God for something that has not yet happened, unless you know in your heart that it's a done deal. That's faith, right?

If you know that God is your Papa Daddy and He is attentive and loving and caring and that you and He are in a perfect, unspoiled relationship that Jesus purchased for you, *then* when a need presents itself, you can thank Him for the answer that is ready to manifest. That is a quantum leap from: "Please God, give us today our daily bread; please fill this need for us." When it comes to needs, this is the way that believers are to pray in the New Covenant. Heaven is open, God is attentive, and He is a Papa who loves us. Thank Him for the answer that is manifesting.

A friend of mine who owns his own business was $80,000 in the hole at the beginning of the year. We would meet for Bible study and we would ask him how things were going, and the report was always disastrous from the flesh perspective (what he could see). But he would always say, "Hey, God's my Father; He's taking care of me, and I have no clue how He's going to do it. But I'm His son and He is prospering me." And in our Bible study we always took time at the end to bless each other and pray for each other. And my friend would never let us pray for a turnaround. His prayer request every week was, "I'm just thanking God for what He is going to do." He meant it. That is faith applied to your needs. What is it really? It is relationship with Papa God. It is being so secure in your sonship that you just know you can count on your Daddy's help. Bam! Contracts, contracts! He's not just out of debt, but God is prospering him.

God is teaching me to pray this way, to pray in new ways. A while ago, I needed a new car. My car had 282,000 miles on it. It's my own fault. When I got this car I blessed it and I told God if He would keep it going, I'd drive it to 300,000 miles. Well, it's hilarious, because it runs great and I have never had it in for service. Everything worked on it. But it started to look kind of rough. Somebody backed into my son when he drove it one day. Someone ran into the side of it when Sherry drove it one day. And then recently, I was following behind some cars in my neighborhood that slowed down in front of me and then stopped. And the person in front of me put her big 'ole Dodge Durango in reverse and backed into the front of my car; bent the hood up and broke the headlamp.

I got it home and started banging the hood down again with a crow bar! And while I'm banging, I'm saying, "God, look at this thing. This is not a good witness. Would you mind terribly if we didn't go to 300,000 miles?" I felt His joy over me. A few months later, I said the same thing and I started thanking Him for a new car. God said to me, "Are you thanking me to try to get me to give you a new car, or are you thanking me because you believe that I've got one for you?" See, sometimes our "thank you's" are just petitions in disguise. Faith in God's goodness and His gift of righteousness helps you pray "thank you for the answer" and really, really deep down believe that God already *has* provided what you need. That comes out of relationship. By the way, I now drive a beautiful new car. And my heart rejoices before the Lord every time I get into it!

I would get thrown out of most churches for saying this, but you know this is right. Stop praying, *"Give us this day our daily bread."* Stop praying like heaven is closed and you have to find a way to open it. Stop praying like God does not see what your needs are and you have to remind Him. Stop praying to Him like you're in some kind of dysfunctional family where the parent doesn't see, doesn't care, and whose arm needs twisted for your needs to be met. Father knows you have need of these things. But you seek to understand the kingdom, the reign, the rule, and the power of God unleashed in you, to understand your sonship and your perfect righteousness, and you will understand that all these things are yours already.

MATTHEW 16 – Part 1

Forbes came out with their pick last year of 2012's 100 Most Powerful People on the planet. The top five in order from the top: (1) Barack Obama, (2) Angela Merkel, Chancellor of Germany, (3) Vladimir Putin, (4) Bill Gates, and (5) Pope Benedict the 16th. According to the doctrine of Papal Supremacy, the Pope enjoys "supreme, full, immediate, and universal power" over the souls of 1.2 billion Catholics around the world. Scripturally, his power is derived based on Jesus' words in Matthew 16. Papal authority: *"On this rock I will build my church* (the rock is understood to be Peter, the first pope)." That's authority. *"The gates of hell shall not prevail against it."* That's power. The pope possesses the keys of the kingdom, so that whatever he loses on earth will be loosed in heaven — power.

This is an important passage; the way you interpret it. This same passage has Jesus saying that the key to binding and loosing, the key to eternal life and being His follower is: *"If anyone desires to come after me, let him deny himself, and take up his cross, and follow me"* (verse 24). And we all know how that has been interpreted — that you have to deny self, you have to crucify yourself. You have to kill the sinner in you, and you have to live the difficult life of self-denial in order to be Jesus' follower and have access to His power.

I want to begin to take a look at these scriptures in Matthew 16 and help you see them in a new light. I believe that if you can receive this message, it will really change the way you see yourself because this is an identity message that Jesus is speaking out. Give yourself a clean slate with these verses. Pretend you haven't had these verses drilled into you since you were ten years old. And as best we can, with fresh eyes, let's allow Jesus to speak for Himself and let this passage speak for itself. I guarantee you, there's power here, more than I was ever taught.

Chapter 16 has 27 verses and it covers a lot of ground (it starts with a run-in with the Pharisees, then it goes into *"Who do people say that I am"* (the dialogue with Peter), and it ends with *"take up your cross and follow me."* But there is only one theme in this chapter. There is one central idea that runs through the whole thing. It is Jesus comparing the flesh with the spirit. It is the flesh way to God versus the spirit way to God, your flesh identity versus your spirit identity, the flesh power to fight evil versus the spirit power to fight evil. Flesh versus spirit. If you see that, you'll get this entire chapter.

It starts right at the beginning of the chapter where Jesus has a run-in with the Pharisees and He ends up calling them hypocrites right to their faces. Look at verse 3: *"Hypocrites! You know how to discern the face of the sky, but you cannot discern the signs of the times."* The signs of the times were the things that showed that God was doing something new right in front of them and they were not recognizing it. Jesus was doing miracles. Those miracles were the signs of the times and the Pharisees needed to take a clue because none of those miracles had ever been done by the Pharisees (followers of the law), but Jesus was doing them. Jesus was on the Forbes' most powerful people, kicking in the gates of hell, showing these signs. And those signs were showing everybody that God was doing business a new way.

The new way was that sinners were welcomed into the kingdom. The old way was that sinners were outcast and had no chance. The new way was that sick people were healed and demons were cast out. There is power available in the new way. The new way was that Gentile believers had access to God just like Jewish believers. The new way was dead people were raised, deaf people could hear, blind people could see, lame people could walk, hungry people could eat, and sinner people could be forgiven before they even asked for it. The woman caught in adultery didn't ask for it. The lame man lowered down from the ceiling didn't ask for it, but Jesus knew what they needed and gave them what they needed before they even asked. That is a new way that ends in power.

But the Pharisees would not admit that God was bringing a new way. They liked the old way. They understood the old way. They were experts of the old way. The old way was that you kept every outward nuance of the law of God (living by your effort, your flesh effort) and you looked holy and people would be so impressed with your holiness. They would be in awe of you, wishing that they could be that holy and that acceptable to God (like those Pharisees). And religious people enjoy that system of *appearing* holy (they still like it today), the system where you try to get in good with God based on your performance in holiness. The Pharisees were leaders of that; they were on the pedestal and they were admired for their holiness.

And then Jesus comes along and He says, *"Unless your righteousness exceeds the righteousness of the scribes and Pharisees, you will by no means enter the kingdom of heaven"* (Matthew 5:20). People are blown away. They have no power in their flesh to be holier than the Pharisees. A few verses later in that same chapter Jesus puts the nail in the coffin of working and trying to earn God's favor and make it to heaven when He says, *"You must be perfect as your heavenly Father is perfect"* (verse 48). They all throw up their hands and say, "It's too hard; no one can do that." Yeah, that's the point! With men, in the flesh, it is impossible, but with God, all things are possible.

Okay, now go back to our passage. Jesus calls the Pharisees hypocrites and then He turns to the disciples and says *"Take heed and beware of the leaven of the Pharisees and the Sadducees"* (verse 6). The disciples don't understand that warning so Jesus has to explain it to them. And in verse 12 they finally get it. Look at verse 12; this is important, this is the theme: *"Then they understood that He did not tell them to beware of the leaven of bread, but of the doctrine of the Pharisees and Sadducees."* What was the doctrine that Jesus says was leaven? It was that your efforts at righteousness put you in a good place with God. Jesus says, "That's wrong." That's leaven. Your efforts in the flesh at holiness are leaven.

If you are relying on your efforts to make things right between you and God, to keep things right between you and God, to get God to like you, to get God to answer your prayer, to be blessed, or to make something happen (to get God to move on your behalf), you have added leaven to your relationship with Him. Our righteousness does not move God to act. If it did, the Pharisees would have seen great miracles. But they had none because the Bible says that our righteousnesses are as filthy rags before God. Notice that it doesn't say our sins are as filthy rags. It says our righteousnesses; the best we can add is as filthy rags. But God has provided a righteousness that has truly made us right with Him, and it is Jesus' righteousness! When we add our own efforts at righteousness, thinking that we are more forgiven when we do well or less forgiven when we sin, we are adding leaven. Beware of the leaven of the Pharisees.

When you make bread, you only need to mix a little bit of leaven into the dough and the whole loaf is leavened. A little leaven leavens the whole loaf. If you are mixing your righteousness into the recipe of how you are saved, and God is mad at you when you mess up and blesses you more when you do something right, you are ruining the whole thing — even if it's just a little bit. It ruins your faith because your faith has become dependent on your performance.

The late Angelo Mitropoulos had a great healing ministry. He would find a person in his healing line who was new to the faith and who had just been healed. Then he would ask that person to pray for someone else right then who needed healing and, many times, that second person would be healed. They would be healed when other believers who had been praying couldn't help them! How could that be? Because the new Christian knows it's *all* God. They know it can't be their own works of righteousness doing anything because they haven't had time to do anything. They haven't been messed up by the church that says, "You do this and this before you think you can pray for a person." The church helps people add leaven. No! Stop!

My grandma used to say, "Too many chefs spoil the soup!" That was her way of saying, "Get out of my kitchen." Too many chefs spoil the soup. You only need one chef — Jesus. You only need one ingredient, and it isn't the works of the flesh. You must "take heed and beware" of the doctrine of the Pharisees (which is work, work, and more work to stay right with God). That was the only doctrine they had.

That doctrine will ruin you. It leaves you condemned and powerless. Trusting your righteousness leaves you powerless. The doctrine of the Pharisees contains no power to free you from sin. It contains no power to kick in the gates of hell. It contains no power to bind and loose spiritual miracles. How many people did the Pharisees miraculously heal? How many guilt ridden hearts did they bind up? None. There was no power there.

Jesus is calling you, just like He was calling the disciples, to give up the leaven. Don't add even a little to your relationship with Jesus or it will ruin the whole loaf. It will ruin God's plan of manifesting His power in you and through you. It's all Jesus' finished work *or* it's you trying to be good enough and never getting there. It is grace found in Jesus' finished work for you or it is you living under the law. Romans 11:6 makes this so clear: *"And if by grace, then it is no longer of works; otherwise grace is no longer grace. But if it is of works, it is no longer grace; otherwise work is no longer work."*

Did you follow that? The Bible says "there is no middle road." You are either made righteous and entitled to God's love and blessings based on grace, the unearned favor Jesus bought you, *or* you are made righteous by your works of righteousness under the law. People want to mix the two, but God doesn't allow it. As a friend of mine says, "Don't be a spiritual bartender and mix together your own drink of law and grace. There is no mixture." Beware of the leaven of the law-doers. Don't mix any of that into your thinking of how God will bless you. You must *know* that you are blessed and perfect in God's sight. He has perfected you in your spirit. That's where the power for life is, the power for binding and loosing, the power for kicking in the gates of hell!!

Power flows from the spirit and not from the flesh. This is exactly what Jesus is telling us in this chapter 16. *"When Jesus came into the region of Caesarea Philippi, He asked His disciples, saying, 'Who do men say that I, the Son of Man, am?' So they said, 'Some say John the Baptist, some Elijah, and others Jeremiah or one of the prophets.' He said to them, 'But who do you say that I am?' Simon Peter answered and said, 'You are the Christ, the Son of the living God.' Jesus answered and said to him, 'Blessed are you, Simon Bar-Jonah, for flesh and blood has not revealed this to you, but my Father who is in heaven. And I also say to you that you are Peter, and on this rock I will build my church, and the gates of Hades shall not prevail against it. And I will give you the keys of the kingdom of heaven, and whatever you bind on earth will be bound in heaven, and whatever you loose on earth will be loosed in heaven'"*— Matthew 16:13-19.

Remember that Jesus is comparing two modes of thought, two approaches to life: the fleshy, man-effort approach to life of the Pharisees, and the spirit, God-effort approach to life; the new and living way. He starts with the flesh (verse 13), *"Who do men say that I, the Son of Man am?"* "Son of Man" is the *earthly* title of Jesus. Jesus is Son of Man and He is Son of God — fully human and fully divine. He is directing them to the earthly title, Son of Man. What He is really asking them is, "Who do people (who are seeing with fleshly eyes) think that I am?" And the answer is logical, it flows out of this. "Well, Jesus, they are seeing your works, which are kind of like the miracle works they've read about with Elijah, and they are saying you are Elijah risen from the dead. And some are hearing how bold you are in your sermons, and you remind them of John the Baptist or a prophet like that."

So if all you knew about Jesus was what you saw and heard in the flesh and you were letting your natural mind inform you about Him, you would say that He is John the Baptist raised from the dead or Elijah come back to earth or a good prophet. You still hear that today. "Jesus was a good prophet." That's how the flesh would inform you when you look at the Son of

Man. *And you would be wrong.* They are wrong. The flesh viewpoint is wrong about Jesus.

Jesus goes on. "But who do *you* say that I am." And Peter says, *"You are the Christ (the Messiah) the Son of the living God."* Yes, Peter. Good! Bravo! You are not seeing with fleshly eyes, you are seeing with spirit eyes. *"Flesh and blood has not revealed this to you,"* Jesus tells him, "and the only way you could know that is if the Father showed that to you. Great job!" It's the distinction between knowing someone after the flesh or knowing them after the spirit. It's the distinction between seeing from human perspective or seeing from the Father's perspective.

To paraphrase, Jesus says, "All right Peter, you understand how people see me in the flesh versus how you see me in the spirit; now let's apply that same principle to you." We're going to start in the flesh. "Blessed are you, Simon Bar-Jonah." That was Peter's *earthly* name — Simon Bar-Jonah. Peter, the disciple, was never called Peter by his mother. Nobody knew him as Peter. They knew him *only* as Simon Bar-Jonah. Simon Bar-Jonah was the name that his mother gave him. When I was a kid and I got in trouble, I knew that it was curtains for me when my mother used my full and formal name. "Gregory Thomas Riether, you get over here now!" That was code for, "Turn around and run like your life depended on it."

Simon Bar-Jonah was Peter's formal given name. It was the name his mother used when he was in trouble. It was on the birth certificate. It was how he was known (how?) *in the flesh.* Jesus is saying, "This is how you are known by *everybody else.*" So if you went to Galilee in Peter's day and said the name "Simon Bar-Jonah, everyone will know: "Oh, yeah, that's that hot headed fisherman, the stubborn guy who cusses up a storm when the catch is bad." That's Simon in the flesh. Now what is Jesus going to do? He is going to give him a new identity.

"And I say to you that you are <u>Petros</u> (that's the Greek for Peter — verse 18)." Petros means "rock" in the Greek; you are Rock Man. Jesus is comparing the two views, the two identities of His disciple. The flesh identity is the identity that everyone knows who grew up with Peter. But Jesus declares to him a new identity, a *spirit* identity. "You are Rock Man. I see who you are in your spirit and it is so different from who you are in the flesh that you need another name." In the flesh, he is Simon Bar-Jonah, cussing fisherman. In the spirit, as God views him, he is Rock Man.

And then Jesus makes a little word play here. He says, "You are Petros (ending r-o-s) and on this petra (ending r-a)," it's not the same, you see. Jesus is not saying that Peter is the rock on which we build the church. He changed the word so that we won't make that mistake. Jesus is saying that on *this concept* the church will be built — the concept of embracing your spirit identity and not your fleshly identity. The spirit identity that the Father reveals is the real identity. As an example, it's not just Jesus, Son of Man. It is Jesus Christ, Son of the Living God. Another example: it's not just Simon Bar-Jonah. It's Rock Man — unmovable, solid, a chip off the old block. It's the Father's view, the spirit reality of the person that *is* the real identity.

What is the concept upon which the church will be built? It is this: *"you must listen to what the Father says about who you are and how you are blessed, and what you can and cannot do in this life."* And Jesus is saying that if you accept the Father's identity of you, your real identity, your spirit identity (not your fleshly identity), you will be unstoppable. You can march right up to the gates of hell, the strongholds of the enemy, and kick down the doors. They will not withstand the power in you. You can bind and you can let loose, you can heal and you can raise from the dead. Nothing will be impossible to you. But you must accept the Father's opinion of you under grace. You must accept that you are a finished work right now in your spirit.

You must reject the leaven, flesh approach that just keeps you condemned and unblessed and fearful of God and without power. You must bathe yourself and train yourself in the finished work of Jesus in you. It is *not* based on your performance in righteousness; it is based on Jesus' performance in righteousness. Depend only on that. God has a new name for you, based on what He sees in the Spirit, based on Christ's finished work, based on Papa's opinion of you.

What is Papa's opinion of you? What is the spirit reality? God says you are totally forgiven. I don't care what you've done or what stupid thing you do today, you are still forgiven. You are completely loved, and you have the Father's heart of love all over you. He will not love you more in heaven than He does right now. He has only love for you. He has only blessings for you. Believe for them on the basis of His love, on the basis of how He sees you; not on the basis of the flesh.

You have a new name, not a name that everyone knows. The name everyone knows brings you no confidence. When that name is called forth, all of the memories of your life in the flesh are called forth; all of your failures, all of your immoralities, all of your stumblings. Jesus has a new name for you based on His finished work. It is untainted by sin, and it is full of the potential that He saw in you when He first knit you in your mother's womb, and He is calling you by that name right now!

Revelations 2:17 says, *"He who has an ear, let him hear what the Spirit says to the churches. To him who overcomes I will give some of the hidden manna to eat. And I will give him a white stone, and on the stone a new name written which no one knows except him who receives it."* Jesus knows your name, your spirit you, your real you. And it is so "you" that when you hear it you will be the only person that that name could fit. No one else could possibly "know it" except you to whom it has been given. That is the name He knows you by right now — beautiful and righteous and perfect and holy and powerful and fearless and honorable and good and upright.

I don't know what that name sounds like. I don't know what it is but you need to go home and look in the mirror and introduce yourself to the true "you," the one that that name represents. It is a name that shows the Father's description of you, the Father's opinion of you. You should, at a minimum, look yourself in the eye and say, "Hello, my name is Greg Riether, and I am the righteous son of the Almighty God."

Don't you think the demons of hell would tremble at someone who knows that is true? Stop cowering as if sickness, disease, failure, tragedy and disappointment have all the power or that the cancer has all the power or your addiction has all the power. They don't have all the power. God has the power, and He has given it to you. Believe this with me, that God has a good plan for you and it does not involve getting kicked around by the devil. It involves you kicking in the gates of hell and not just pulling people out of there, but declaring that that territory once belonging to Satan has now become the possession of Jesus. We are expanding the reign and rule of Jesus in this world.

We are calling out the hypocrisy in the church that mixes our flesh self with our spirit self. The only thing that matters is the new creation that you truly are in Jesus. And my friend, if you mess up and fall into sin, we will remind you of your true identity, your righteous self that Jesus has already made you. I just want to keep pulling out of you and helping you see the righteous person you already are in God's eyes because the Father has made a declaration about you. And if the Father says a thing is so — it is so!

You are not Simon Bar-Jonah. You are not known by God in the flesh. You are Peter. You are Rock Man! Who is the real you? It's not the fleshly you with your failures. It's the new creation you. Hello, my name is _____, and I am the righteous son of the Almighty God!

MATTHEW 16 – Part 2

"Jesus answered and said to him, 'Blessed are you, Simon Bar-Jonah, for flesh and blood has not revealed this to you, but my Father who is in heaven. And I also say to you that you are Peter, and on this rock I will build my church, and the gates of Hades shall not prevail against it. And I will give you the keys of the kingdom of heaven, and whatever you bind on earth will be bound in heaven, and whatever you loose on earth will be loosed in heaven.'"— Matthew 16:17-19

The whole point of this passage is that Jesus is trying to get across this idea of flesh versus spirit. Flesh identity (who do men say that I, the Son of Man am — Jesus' flesh identity, people's flesh interpretation of His identity). "You are Elijah; you are John the Baptist raised from the dead; you are a great prophet." That is still how unbelievers see Jesus — as a good man, a great prophet. The flesh identity versus His spirit identity; which is — "you are the Christ, *the* Son of the living God." Jesus — "very good, Peter, for flesh hasn't revealed this to you, but my Father who is in heaven."

Then Jesus applies the lesson to Peter. He says to him, "You are Simon Bar-Jonah" — that is your flesh identity, that is what everyone calls you — Simon, cussing fisherman. It doesn't say he was a cussing fisherman, but in Simon's own words when he was called by Jesus to follow Him, Simon said, "Depart from me, Lord, for I am a sinful man." That was Simon's own sense of his identity before God; Simon Bar-Jonah, "a sinful man before you, Lord." So Jesus says, "You are Simon Bar-Jonah," (flesh identity) but I say to you that you are Peter (which means Rock). I say to you that you are Rock Man." It is a new identity. In the flesh, that's not who he was. Jesus is seeing something that Peter is not seeing and giving him a name that fits what He sees. This is how God sees him. It is who he is in the spirit. He is not Simon Bar-Jonah; he is Rock Man before the Lord.

Notice that Peter doesn't give himself the new identity; Jesus gives it to him. See, you are not earning your identity before God. Jesus gives to you your new spirit identity. It is the reality of who you are before God. It is God's opinion of you, and it is given to you as a gift and not a title that you have to earn or work toward. It is Papa's view of you right now and it is in effect immediately.

Peter did not have to wait for this name (this new identity) to become a reality. It wasn't like somewhere down the line this would become a reality for Peter, something that he will take on in the future, and then folks are going to look back at him and be impressed and name cathedrals after him. No, Jesus put this in the present tense. "I say to you, you are Rock Man, right now; that is who you truly are."

Do you see how powerful that is? Do you see that your new spirit identity is in effect right this very minute? You don't earn it, you don't grow into it, and you don't wait for it to materialize. You may not feel like you are (in reality) this beautiful, solid, powerful, loved, perfected person that Jesus says you are. It is real regardless of how you feel. Really, the only thing you can do is accept it or reject it. You accept your spirit identity that Jesus gives to you as a gift and receive that as the identity out of which you live, or you reject it and keep seeing yourself as John Doe, the screw-up, John Doe, the sinner, John Doe, the one who wants to live right for God but who can't ever please God.

No, you have to deny that flesh identity. Jesus said, "If you want to follow after me, you must deny that identity." You have to consider that identity to be crucified with Him. You are the spirit identity that Jesus gave to you. You are righteous, holy, worthy, qualified, forgiven forever, forgiven today, tomorrow, next week, next month, and forever. You are in a constant state of forgiveness, in a constant state of righteousness. You are pleasing to God, perfected in your spirit, eternally redeemed, and the beloved son in whom Papa is already pleased. Jesus declares this: "I say to you, you are a new identity in me (I have given it to you). You are the person on a firm foundation; you are Rock Man (because you are on me)!"

So you have this new identity that stands in contradiction to the flesh identity. What do you do with the flesh identity? Jesus said you utterly deny it; you deny its place in your thinking, you crucify it in your mind. *"If anyone desires to come after me let him deny himself, take up his cross, and follow me"* (verse 24). You deny it and crucify it in your mind. The flesh identity is not your true identity. And if you can get that right, then heaven's power is available to you, the gates of hell will not prevail against you, and you plunder the enemy. You kick in hell's gates and steal back people from its grip (you declare their freedom) and move them from Hades (which means the place of the dead). You move people from death to life.

And, Jesus says, on this principle of spirit identity, He gives to you the keys of the kingdom of heaven (verse 19): *"And whatever you bind on earth will be bound in heaven and whatever you loose on earth will be loosed in heaven."* The keys to the kingdom of heaven are access to heaven. We have to get this concept that

Jesus is getting across to us. It's your spirit identity that is linked to God — *not your flesh identity.*

If you come to God on the basis of who you are in the flesh, you will not partake of the goodness and power of God. The typical church has trained us to come to God on the basis of our flesh identity, our Simon Bar-Jonah identity. I used to train people through worship and through teaching on prayer that they must admit that they are sinners and confess that sin to God and get the sin under the blood. That is coming in our Simon Bar-Jonah identity, our "depart from me Lord, for I am a sinner" identity. Jesus is teaching a radical new thought. That is not who you are. You relate to God by your spirit.

This was a mystery to me for the longest time. Do you remember the story of Jesus talking to the Samaritan woman at the well? And she says, *"We worship God on this mountain, but you Jews says that God should be worshipped in Jerusalem." And Jesus answers her, "But the hour is coming, and now is, when the true worshippers will worship the Father in spirit and truth, for the Father is seeking such to worship Him. God is Spirit, and those who worship Him must worship in spirit and truth"* (John 4:23-24). This has mystified a lot of people. How do you worship God in spirit?

You know worship is a form of prayer. Worship is communication with God, communion with God, adoration of God, being loved by God and loving God back. It is connecting to the living God. How do you do that? You do that in your spirit. God is spirit, Jesus says, and those who worship Him must worship in spirit and truth (truth engages the mind — spirit and truth). What that means is that you must come to Him on the basis of your spirit identity. Jesus said, "This is who you are." This is the truth of who you are before

God. You are Rock Man, forgiven and free, beloved son of the Father. Worshipping in spirit is worshipping the Father out of that reality. It is boldly coming to the throne of grace because you are forgiven and loved. It is not groveling up to God like a failed human being that He is angry with. God is not angry with you. He is never angry with you. That is one of the planks of the New Covenant (Isaiah 54:9).

I truly believe that this is the key to joyful, victorious life in Christ. It is receiving your new identity; *that* is a spirit reality. Your new identity of being righteous and acceptable and worthy is not something you can see and taste and touch and feel; it is not a thing of the flesh. In fact, the flesh (in its sin and failures) tries to negate your spirit reality and the flesh condemns you. To accept who you are in the spirit, you have to know what God says about you and agree with it. The spirit identity is based on God's truth-telling about you. You have to believe that what God says about you is true. You are Rock Man. You are not Simon Bar-Jonah. (I think it would be easier if we all just got new names!) Somehow we have to make our primary identity the identity that Jesus gave us. And *that* is an identity of the spirit.

The issue on this planet is that our lives are wrapped around the flesh. The whole horizon of our existence is based on "what shall we eat, what shall we drink, how shall we be clothed, look at what I *did*, look at what I didn't *do*." We are grounded in the flesh. We make all our provisions for the flesh. But the flesh reality does not give you access to heaven. God relates by spirit because He is Spirit. We need to change the way we see ourselves. And it's not just accepting the truth about what Jesus did for us on the cross; forgiven forever. That is fantastic truth, but those relating to God must come in spirit and in truth.

You must come in spirit. You must see yourself as a spirit being. You are not a flesh and blood being. You are a spirit being that occupies a flesh and blood vehicle. This flesh and blood is not me. If this body is me, then I have a problem because this is going to wear out and die. But Jesus said that this is not me. As I preach, the bodies that I see occupying the chairs are not the core of you. I cannot see the real you. That's why Jesus could say to Mary and Martha, "Those who live and believe in me will never die." That is a true statement that applies to every believer. You will never die. But that is not true if your identity is your flesh. You will answer, "Yes, I will die because we all die." Not me! You can kill this body but you can't kill me.

You are not that body that I see. I am not this body. I am a spirit being that inhabits a body. This body is limited, it is finite, it can succumb to the toxins of this world, it can get sick, it wears out, and it is corruptible and passing away. Paul says in 1 Corinthians 15 that on the last day that this corruptible will put on incorruptibility and this mortal will put on immortality. That's what this flesh reality is like; corruptible and mortal. But my spirit is not like my flesh. My spirit is perfect and incorruptible. *"By one offering, He has perfected forever those who are being made holy"* (Hebrews 10:14).

You are perfected forever in your spirit and from the platform of that perfected spirit, you have communion with God. Your spirit is not limited in any way. In fact, your spirit is your direct connection to the infinite. Your body does not touch heaven, but your spirit is seated with Christ right now in the heavenlies. That is an awesome truth about your spirit. Your spirit has been made one with Jesus' spirit, and in your spirit you have a direct, unbreakable, connection to God — a connection to infinite power, infinite wisdom; the infinite! One of the things that God has been teaching me is to live life out of my spirit identity, my spirit self, and not my flesh identity, my flesh self. It's a matter of reprogramming our thinking. It's not something you do. It's something you realize.

Adam and Eve were spirit beings that inhabited a body. They were not bodies that had life, like the rest of the creatures on the earth. But God breathed into Adam and Eve His own Spirit, and His Spirit was the life of man. And as they lived life, they related to God (who was Spirit) in an intimate way. They walked with God and talked with God in the cool of the evening. They were relating to God by their spirit identities — the only thing they knew.

It wasn't until the fall of man, when they fell into sin, that they even took notice of their bodies, and they saw that they were naked. Before then, the glory of the Lord had been their covering. The glory of the Lord is His own Spirit self, manifested on them. All they knew how to do was relate to God by their spirit selves, their real selves. And when they fell into sin, they suddenly took note of the lesser reality, their flesh and blood selves, and they noted their nakedness. From then on, our flesh identity has been the primary focus for how we live. But there is no power in that. The life of God doesn't flow from that. It's your spirit identity that is your connection to God and it is your connection to every spiritual blessing in the heavenlies.

Ephesians 1:3 says that God has "*blessed us with every spiritual blessing in the heavenlies in Christ.*" Every blessing that God has for you comes to you in spiritual form. Healing is a spiritual blessing. Prosperity is a spiritual blessing. And this is exactly what Jesus meant when He said that on this concept of your spirit identity, you could kick in the gates of hell. And He also said (verse 19), "*I give to you the keys of the kingdom; whatever you bind of earth will be bound in heaven, and whatever you loose on earth will be loosed in heaven."*

I will tell you exactly what that means. You will want to write it in your Bible and look it up for yourself and see if I am right about this. Jesus is talking about how you, a spirit being, can bring the supernatural power of heaven into the physical, on this earth. And this teaching of Jesus, on binding and loosing, has been so confused and misinterpreted that weird doctrines have come out of this. It comes from the confusion of the translations. Young's literal translation of this verse is the only one that I've found that just interprets the Greek word-for-word here. Jesus puts two verbs together, but only one of them ever seems to get translated because if you translate both verbs together, it's awkward. And the translators didn't know what to do with it.

But let me open this up to you. Jesus said, "Whatever you bind on earth; and then right here is a future form of the verb "to be." So it should read, "whatever you bind on earth shall be." And then Jesus put a second verb, in a completely different tense — the perfect passive tense which carries the sense of completion. Young's literal gets this right and it comes out this way: *"Whatever you bind on earth shall be, having been bound in heaven; and whatever you loose on earth shall be, having been loosed in heaven."*

Jesus is talking about accessing His finished work in heaven, accessing what has already been bound and loosed in heaven, and bringing it to the earth in physical (flesh) form. *"Whatever you bind on earth shall be* (shall come into existence here), *having been bound in heaven* (by me). *And whatever you loose on earth shall be* (shall come into existence here) *having been loosed in heaven."* In heaven, healing has been bought and paid for. It is a spirit reality. When you go to God in spirit and truth (in your spirit identity, your Rock Man identity), you have access to every spiritual blessing. You access the infinite, you access the spiritual. And what is teaching us to do to speak forth on earth that spiritual blessing, speaking it forth into this physical world. "I lose healing into you in Jesus' name. I lose prosperity upon you in Jesus' name." You speak out of your spirit identity, the identity that accesses the things of heaven — the blessings that Jesus accomplished on the cross.

"Whatever you bind on earth shall be." Interestingly, the gospel of Matthew may have actually been written originally in both the Greek and the Hebrew languages. There are very ancient Hebrew manuscripts of Matthew's Gospel. And what this verse says in the Hebrew is not, *"I will give you the keys of the kingdom and whatever you bind,* etc." It says, *"I will give you utterances, and whatever you bind on earth shall be."* The way you bind and loose is through the tongue. You speak out heaven's reality, accessing heaven by your spirit identity, and what you speak out shall be, having already been bought and paid for by Jesus.

And that's exactly what this means. This really requires a different mindset about how you see yourself because you have been given great authority and access through your spirit identity. I can hear people telling me, "Well, pastor, we are flesh and blood beings. We are both flesh and blood *and* spirit beings" And I agree with you. When the body is miserable, you're miserable. The problem is that as soon as you give equal weight to flesh and spirit, the spirit identity loses because everything around you reinforces the flesh self, the flesh needs, the flesh weaknesses. What shall we eat, what shall we drink? I am cold, I am hot, look at how I behave, on and on and on. The whole world instructs you on your flesh identity. Only Jesus says, *"Seek first the kingdom of God and His righteousness* (righteousness as a gift; righteousness as an identity) *and all these things will be added to you."*

Just let me help you get your head around this. Say this out loud: "I am a spirit being. I have a flesh body. My spirit identity is my true identity. My spirit is connected to Jesus. I am in Him. He is in me. My spirit is perfect, and I possess God's righteousness. He gave it to me as a gift. I am seated with Christ in the heavenlies. I am connected to heaven right now. I am touching the infinite. I have access to every spiritual blessing. They belong to me. My spirit is touching them. I can lose these blessings into my life. God wants me to lose them. Jesus told me to lose them because He loves me and they belong to me. I lose healing into my body. I lose my healing. I lose healing into my heart. I lose healing into my muscles. I lose healing into my bones and into my skin. I am accessing heaven. Jesus gave me the keys. They belong to me."

"I lose prosperity into my home. I lose financial independence into my home. I lose more than I need into my household so I can be a blessing and because Papa loves me. I lose prosperity into my children and my children's children to the thousandth generation. My children will prosper. I lose healing in my psyche. I lose healing in my mind. I am bathed in Papa's love. He sees me right now and He loves me. I am free of my past mistakes. I am forgiven forever. My mind is quiet. My heart is full. My joy is abundant. He satisfies me with good things. I lose good things and great satisfaction upon my life. Jesus said I could do this, so I am doing this. And what I have loosed today shall be, having been loosed in heaven already by Jesus."

EATING WITH SINNERS

"As Jesus passed on from there, He saw a man named Matthew sitting at the tax office. And He said to him, "Follow Me." So he arose and followed Him. Now it happened, as Jesus sat at the table in the house that, behold, many tax collectors and sinners came and sat down with Him and His disciples. And when the Pharisees saw it, they said to His disciples, 'Why does your Teacher eat with tax collectors and sinners?' When Jesus heard that, He said to them, 'Those who are well have no need of a physician, but those who are sick. But go and learn what this means: 'I desire mercy and not sacrifice,' for I did not come to call the righteous, but sinners, to repentance." — Matthew 9:9-12

This passage is your guide map and help in hunting down and killing a few sacred cows. In Matthew 9, the lame man was brought to Jesus, and Jesus forgave the man all his sins without the man's consent. The man never said he was sorry, never asked Jesus for forgiveness, never made confession of his sin, and never worked his way to an altar in tears. He just got in the presence of Jesus and Jesus said to him, "Your sins are forgiven you." The religious people were deeply offended. Why? Because Jesus circumvented the religious system for getting yourself clean, the system that they had invested their whole lives in and that defined their relationship with God. He made forgiveness way too easy. He made it an act of grace.

God forgives people without their consent. He forgave you without your consent. In fact, God has already forgiven the entire world and is no longer in the forgiving business. He forgave you once, and He is not forgiving you again. He did that over 2,000 years ago when Jesus took the sins of the entire world onto Himself. The Book of Hebrews says in chapter 10 that after He made that sacrifice He sat down. The forgiveness work is done. Our job is to speak it out to people so they can believe in Jesus and have Eternal Life.

Jesus offends the religious people by dispensing grace; unearned, unmerited, way too easy forgiveness. The religious people get mad. But wait; Jesus is not done offending them yet. He leaves that place, walks on a little bit, and people are following Him to see what He's going to do next. He looks around to find the most despicable, underhanded, despised, loathsome, sinful person He can find. He sees Matthew the tax collector, sitting in his tax booth. Perfect. Perfect. You couldn't get more low-life than a tax collector. The fact that Matthew was in a tax booth tells us exactly the *kind* of tax collector he was. He was "*mokhes;*" he collected taxes by the road and taxed commerce; any kind of commerce. If it moved on wheels he could tax it. And he could virtually set his own rates. It was a racket. To pass by on the road, Matthew would make you pay. He gave a portion to the Romans, and kept the rest himself. It was pure profit. If someone refused to pay or caused trouble, Matthew had Roman soldiers available to strong-arm people, rough them up a bit, and scare them into paying.

If there's an equivalent to the modern day Mafia, this is it. Tax collectors were hated, for good reason. They were religiously unclean, they couldn't enter the temple, they were outcasts, and were universally despised. Jesus, with this crowd in-tow, locks eyes with Matthew, this little scammer, this low-life, widow-cheating puke of a man, and says to him, "Follow me. Let's take a walk. Let's hang out." We don't know the conversation because it's not recorded, but at some point Matthew says to Jesus, "Why don't you come to my house for dinner?" And Jesus accepts the invitation.

And the people gasp. All the people gasp. Normal people gasp. Religious people gasp. Everybody gasps. And you would have gasped too. I cannot paint this picture in a way that would make it as offensive to you as it really was when Jesus sat down and ate dinner with Matthew and his scamming Mafia low-life friends. To eat with a person in Jesus' day was to say, "You and I have a friendship."

The people, the religious people especially, would have been choking. If they had recognized Jesus' identity as the Son of the Living God, they would have been doubly choking. Everybody knows that God cannot hang out with sinners. He can't do it. His nature won't allow it. God doesn't fellowship with unholy vessels. "God is a holy God." He cannot fellowship with sinner people. He cannot hang out with unworthy, unrepentant, people. Why? Because He is holy.

If you ask religious people to define the nature of God in one word, most people, upon reflection, would say that God is holy. He reveals Himself as a holy God. The angels fly about the throne looking at God and they never cease to say, "Holy, holy, holy." I agree with you that God is a holy God. But most people, when they say that God is holy, mean that He is squeaky clean. American holiness means morality; it means sinlessness. If you go to a church that has "holiness" in its name (e.g., Pentecostal Holiness) you will find a church that defines holiness as moral cleanliness. The Americanized version of moral cleanliness is women don't cut their hair, they don't wear jewelry, they don't wear makeup, they have to wear skirts, but not skirts that are too short, the men have to wear long sleeves, no movies, no dancing, no smoking, and no drinking. Why? Because we are holy as God is holy.

No, that is not holiness. God is holy. But holiness has nothing to do with morality. I liked Jeff Turner's definition of holiness: "Holiness means weirdness. It literally means "otherness." God is other. He is so other, that the angels see new other-ness all the time and it blows them away. Say it this way, God exists and interacts in ways that are not like the ways un-regenerated humans would interact. God loves His enemies. That does not make sense to angels. God loves sinner people. That makes no sense to angels. God does not deal with people according to their iniquities. That makes no sense to angels. And it makes no sense to un-regenerated people. Un-regenerated people (and even believers whose minds are un-regenerated) think that God is going "to get" people based on their wickedness. But God is not like that. He is weird. Do you know what makes Him so weird? It's love.

The New Testament disclosure of God defines God by another word. The primary characteristic of God is not that He is holy; *the primary characteristic of God is that He is love.* The Bible says that to know God is to know love. 1 John 4:8 — *"He who does not love does not know God, for God is love."* To know God, to understand God, is to know that He is all about love. Every action is motivated by love. He does not act apart from love. He has perfect love for you. And your sin does not affect His love at all.

This is one of the sacred cows of Christianity — that your sin affects God's ability to hang out with you, and, in fact affects *His desire* to hang out with you. That is all wrong. Go back to Adam and Eve. The common misperception of this story is that Adam and Eve sinned by eating the forbidden fruit and God saw that they had sinned. He got mad at them, tossed them out of the Garden of Eden as punishment, and was unable to fellowship with them because *now* they were in a fallen state. Wrong!

Adam and Eve did sin. And right after they sinned, God came to them just like He always did and He called out "Adam, where are you?" Before the fall, Adam and Eve had an intimate love relationship; they were naked before God and God was naked before them and there was no shame — just uninhibited love. He would come to the garden and they would come running to Him, to share in His love, to love and be loved. Humanity, made in his image, was an extension of His family. God as Father, Son and Holy Spirit loved one another in perfect harmony, and the trinity created you and me to share in the love of the Godhead.

When Adam sinned, God's love was not interrupted. God knew that Adam had sinned. And what was His response? His response was to come to the garden just like He always did, to have fellowship with His children. The sin was not a hindrance that kept God from being able to love us. The sin did not affect God's desire or ability to love. But what it did was break something in our thinking. It injected guilt and shame into our psyche, and the guilt and shame caused us to run from God. God did not run from us. We ran from God. We hid ourselves from Him, but God's love was unbroken. He never stopped loving us, even in our sin.

He makes them clothing, and yes, he removes them from the Garden of Eden, but why? He does it so that they will not eat of the tree of life and live forever in a fallen state. God's love never wavered. God still wanted us to receive His love, but our guilt and shame kept us in hiding. We thought God was mad, and we think God is still mad. The good news is "God is not mad at you." He loves you. Receive his love. That is His goal for you — to get you to a place where you can partake of the love of the Godhead family where you can receive His love and where you can join the love circle and love Him back.

If you think that your sin changes God's opinion of you, changes the way He can relate to you, changes the way He *wants* to relate to you, you don't know God. Stop making an idol of sin. Stop believing that your sin makes you unlovable to Him. Sin is not like kryptonite to God, like Superman who couldn't be in its presence. God doesn't comes into the room and say, "I . . . can't . . . take . . . it; just . . . too . . . much . . . sin, I . . have . . . to . . . leave. It . . . might . . . get . . . on . . . me." That's not it. That's a wrong view of sin and a wrong view of God.

God loves people — all people. And Jesus showed us how God interacts with people in sin. He doesn't keep away from them; He seeks them out and fellowships with them. He sought out Matthew and all his parasitic, slimy, cheating friends and He fellowshipped with them. He laughed with them. He disclosed the kingdom to them. He showed them and told them what God was really like. Did God approve of their sin? No. But the antidote to sin is not a list of rules to follow. Matthew and his friends had been given that list, they knew that list, and it did not help them. The antidote to sin is fellowship with God. You get around God, you start partaking of his love, and the result is that you start looking like your heavenly Papa. You start loving like God loves when you start experiencing His love for you. Here's the thing, you have to start getting some idea of your value to your heavenly Papa. Most of us don't know our value very well.

Jesus once described you as a precious coin that was lost. He said a woman had ten coins and one of her coins got lost. The moment Adam and Eve sinned was the moment God lost the coin. And listen to God's heart in this. The woman was not content to say, "Well, I've still got nine other coins." No, she goes on an all-out hunt and she is not going to stop until she finds what she lost. Why? Why does she do that? Because the coin is valuable. It has value. It is precious. And the fact that it has fallen in the dirt doesn't make it less valuable. Just because the coin falls into the dirt doesn't make the coin dirt. It is just as valuable in the dirt as it was out of the dirt. It has the same value and it possesses the same intrinsic worth whether it is dirty or not.

Jesus says in that parable that the woman lights a lamp and she sweeps the house. The houses of Jesus' day were dirt floor houses. So this woman is getting down on her hands and her knees and sifting through the dirt. The dirt doesn't intimidate her at all. Her hands are in it, her knees are in it; the woman goes down to the place where the coin is, just like the Son of God goes down to the place where we are. He came to earth to do what? Seek and save that which was lost to Him. That's you. And when He found you, He rejoiced. Why? Because you were valuable to him. You are so valuable.

I am not the worm that my denominational heritage said I was. You're not the worm your denomination said you were. God does not define you by the dirt. You didn't go from being a precious coin to a worm when you fell into sin. You are still precious. God is not in the least intimidated by your sin, He is not intimidated by your guilt, He is not intimidated by your shame, and He is not intimidated by your filth. He looks at you, even when you're in the middle of your sin, and loves you without judgment or condemnation. That is the power of His love for you. That is the power of what Jesus did for you.

We don't understand that, so we stay hiding from God and His love. We say stupid things in prayers like, "Oh God, we are not worthy of your love, we are not worthy of your blessings." No. Wrong. The Godhead is not stupid. What we mean when we say "we are not worthy" is "we are not worth it." We are not worth Jesus coming and dying. This is a fat, ugly, religious cow that keeps you from relishing in the love of Papa God. And that cow has got to die. Jesus thought you were worth it. Who are you to say He was wrong? In fact, Paul the Apostle presented the good news of Jesus once to a Jewish audience and they could not receive his message. And he says to them, *"It was necessary that the word of God should be spoken to you first; but since you reject it, and do not see yourselves worthy of everlasting life, behold, we turn to the Gentiles"* (Acts 13:46).

The religious mind has been programmed to believe that we are not worthy. But God thought that you were worthy of His love even when you didn't love Him back. The dirt doesn't make you dirt. The dirt doesn't detract from your value. The second member of the trinity, Jesus Himself, sought out and hung with women who sold their bodies for sex, with scammers like Matthew and Zaccheaus who cheated little old ladies out of their last penny. Why? Is it because they are worms? No, it's because they are coins. They are valuable. You are valuable. And even in your sin, Jesus loves you. Jesus likes hanging out with you. He wants you to know how loved you are by the whole trinity — Papa, Son, Holy Spirit. They want to pour love into you so that you quit hiding behind self-effort and religious facades, so that you will know your worth and enter into the circle of love that is the Godhead.

So Jesus finds Matthew; scammer, scheming Matthew. And the Son of God, God Himself, sat down with Matthew and all his sinner friends and had dinner. And He loved on him and told him what God was really like. And scammer, scheming Matthew was never the same.

And the religious people looked on and said, "Why does He eat with tax-collectors and sinners?" And Jesus said, *"Those who are well have no need of a physician, but those who are sick. But go and learn what this means; I desire mercy and not sacrifice. For I did not come to call the righteous, but sinners to repentance* (to change their mind about God) — to undo the infected thinking that God is mad and that you are unworthy of His love."

"Those who are sick need a physician." Ask a religious person what the sickness is and they will tell you it is sin. Sin is the sickness. No, sin is not the sickness. Sin is a symptom of the sickness. The sickness is the broken part of us that runs from God's love and that keeps us from being able to receive it.

Jesus tells religious people (people who are working hard to keep themselves acceptable to God by doing religious things), *"Go and learn what this means — 'I desire mercy and not sacrifice.'"* Jesus was quoting Hosea 6:6 in the Old Testament. The Old Testament word for grace is *"chesed."* Oftentimes it is translated as "loving-kindness." In Hosea 6:6 God says, "I desire *chesed*, and not sacrifice." I desire grace, not sacrifice. Sacrifice is what you would do to make yourself acceptable to God. It is an outward religious practice. That's not what God wants. He doesn't want to relate to us based on outward religious practices. He wants to relate to us based on grace, unearned favor. The heart of grace is love.

Papa is saying, "Just let me love you. My heart's desire is *chesed*. I want to pour loving kindness and grace into you. I want you to know what it's like to swim in the ocean of my love. You are worth it. You are the pearl of great price. You are a precious coin I lost 6,000 years ago. You were lost and couldn't find your way back to me. But I came for you. And I got on my hands and knees in the dirt and I found you. And I rejoiced when I found you. And I cleaned you and put you back with me. And I will never lose you again. And all I have for you is love. I love you."

FASTING – Matthew 9

"Then the disciples of John came to Him, saying, "Why do we and the Pharisees fast often, but your disciples do not fast?" And Jesus said to them, 'Can the friends of the bridegroom mourn as long as the bridegroom is with them? But the days will come when the bridegroom will be taken away from them, and then they will fast. No one puts a piece of un-shrunk cloth on an old garment; for the patch pulls away from the garment, and the tear is made worse. Nor do they put new wine into old wineskins, or else the wineskins break, the wine is spilled, and the wineskins are ruined. But they put new wine into new wineskins, and both are preserved." — Matthew 9:14-17

"The disciples of John came to Him saying, 'Why do we and the Pharisees fast often, but your disciples do not fast'" (verse 14)? These are the disciples of John the Baptist who come to Jesus, and they want to know why Jesus and His disciples are not participating in the religious practice of fasting, or going without food. This is a religious fast.

At one point in my life, I participated in religious fasting. I was serious about fasting. I wrote a little booklet on fasting (that no one is permitted to ever read because it's all wrong!). I did three-day fasts, seven-day fasts, twenty-one day fasts. I did forty-day fasts. In fact, I had years as a Lutheran when I would fast from Ash Wednesday (the beginning of Lent) to Resurrection Sunday. That wasn't just a forty-day fast; it was a forty-six day fast. I was better, you see. I was an over-achiever. I would just drink juice and nothing else. I didn't do wimpy "Daniel fasts." Part of it was the bragging rights, but you have to do it subtly. You can't get caught bragging; but you can squeeze it into a conversation. "I fast better. I fast longer than you."

I like to win. If you ever play Monopoly with me, you'll find out. No mercy. I would make my kids cry when they were little and I would beat them at Monopoly. "You landed on Park Place, you are out. Sorry, I win, you lose." I was an over-achiever and I would fast like an over-achiever. Fasting is miserable. Long fasts are miserable and dangerous. So I was miserable, and fasted like a maniac. I fasted to "win." I would get upset at people who would not fast with me or who wouldn't consider doing even a shorter fast because I thought, "I am working hard at getting close to God and I'm miserable, and I think everybody ought to be as miserable as I am."

We can all be miserable together trying to get close to God, trying to get our lives under control, trying to get God to move, trying to get holier in order to hear some special word from God. I'll try double hard to make sure that my motives toward people are pure; no greed, no envy, no anger, no lust, just calm misery. If you do everything right, Isaiah 58:9 says, *"Then you shall call, and the Lord will answer, you shall cry, and He will say, 'Here I am.'"* See, that was the goal — to meet up with God. God would say, "Here I am." I wanted God to say, "Here I am!!" I felt far from Him. It took work to get close to Him. He had to see that I was serious about wanting Him because only those who search with *all* their heart and *all* their strength will find Him.

Okay, that's all wrong. Fasting is part of the Old Covenant relationship that Israel had with God. It is not part of the New Covenant relationship that you have with Papa. I realize that this statement makes some people mad; but let me make a case because Jesus has something for us that far exceeds fasting as a way to demonstrate to yourself that your flesh does not have dominance over you.

We think in the Old Testament that the people were all about fasting. Everybody did it all the time. God required it often and it was a way to get close to God. Do you know that the truth is that God only required it one time a year from His people? Leviticus 16:29-30: *"This shall be a statute forever for you: In the seventh month, on the tenth day of the month, you shall afflict your souls and do no work at all, whether a native of your own country or a stranger who dwells among you. For on that day the priest shall make atonement for you, to cleanse you that you may be clean from all your sins before the LORD."* That phrase, "you shall afflict your souls," is a euphemism for fasting. The Hebrew word for "souls" there also means "appetites." So you can see how they get fasting from this; you are to afflict your appetite.

This is the only place in the Law of Moses where fasting is specifically required of God's people. And on what day was this fast required by the Lord? The Day of Atonement, the day when the sins of the entire nation were atoned for by the priest's sacrifice offering. And what the people were saying by their fasting was "we are lacking." There is something lacking in us. Our souls are hungry for righteousness just like our bodies are hungry right now for food. Our souls long to be satisfied.

Recently, when I was reading and meditating on this, I had a really neat experience. I had a strong word from the Holy Spirit, where the Spirit said to me, "Greg, the fasting in the Old Testament is a picture of the people's lack in every area of their lives." They were doing it because God told them to do it, but God had them fast in order to be a picture for us of lack. And the picture doesn't end with fasting (lack). On the Day of Atonement the people would fast. What was the remedy to the fast (lack)? Well, they stop fasting after the atonement is made. After the sacrifice for sin is made, after the lamb is sacrificed, the lack is gone. You stop fasting. You start feasting. It's a picture. When Jesus comes, the lack is gone.

Now in Israel, the religious practice of fasting expanded rapidly as something "holy" that you could do. And people went on fasts and longer fasts. They tore their clothes and covered themselves with ashes, and it became part of the regular routine of religious life so that Pharisees would fast two or three days out of every week. The disciples of John did the same thing. When John's disciples came up to Jesus they said, "How come we and the Pharisees fast often (all the time!!), but you guys don't ever fast?"

There was only one time in the entire ministry of Jesus that He fasted, and it was when He went out into the wilderness. That's at the beginning of His ministry. What's going on in the beginning of His ministry? Jesus is baptized for sins in the Jordan. Does Jesus have sins He needs baptized or washed from? No, He is taking your place. He is repenting of your sins, taking the bath for you, in your place. Then what happens? He goes out into the wilderness to be tempted of the devil. He is tempted in every way, taking your temptations. While He is out there, He fasts for forty days. The number forty represents a trial that ends in grace. Forty days of rain with Noah that ends with a new covenant and new start. Forty years of Israel in the wilderness that ends in the Promised Land. Jesus fasts for forty days in the wilderness. He suffers our time of lack, our lives of neediness. And when the forty days are done, that period of lack is over. He takes the lack for you.

And He comes back from the wilderness and dispenses His supply everywhere He goes. For people who are hungry; He feeds them miraculously, more than enough. For people who are sick; He heals them with miracle cures. For people who are caught in sin; He forgives them with miracle forgiveness, unearned forgiveness. They are given forgiveness apart from them being miserable and paying their dues, apart from misery, apart from fasting. Jesus did it for you. The lack is done. It is time for supply.

"Why do you and your disciples not fast and we and the Pharisees fast all the time?" Because the picture of lack is done. There's a new picture in town, and it's of sufficiency. The object of the fast for Isaiah was: *"You shall call, and the Lord will answer, you shall cry, and He will say, 'Here I am.'"* If you got to that place in your fast where God was saying, "Here I am," then you made it. You arrived, because to have God show up and pay attention to you was the answer to your fast, the answer to your lack. The goal to the fast was not just that a little prayer got answered. The goal of the fast was God saying, "Here I am."

So Jesus says, *"Can the friends of the bridegroom mourn as long as the bridegroom is with them?"* In other words, why would you fast if the goal of your fasting is standing right in front of you? "Here I am." The Bridegroom is here. The disciples are with Jesus, and they have everything they need. Nobody is getting sick; everyone is getting healed. We have plenty to eat, plenty to support ourselves, and He is telling us we are clean and forgiven (that God has our sin covered). He is convincing us of our righteousness. We are experiencing Papa God's love. The Lord is my shepherd, I suffer no lack." If I suffer no lack, why would I need to fast? God is saying, "Here I am."

That is the good news of Jesus. Apart from your religious efforts, you have God's attention. Apart from your religious fasting and church-going, apart from begging God or doing *anything, anything* to try to get God to show up, He shows up. In fact, it's better than that. It's way better than that. The work that Jesus accomplished made it way better than God just showing up when you need Him. It's totally different from the Old Testament. God is not going to relate to people the way He related to people under the Old Covenant Law. There is going to be a short intermission of three days, and then all heaven is going to break loose.

Jesus says, *"But the days will come when the bridegroom will be taken away from them, and then they will fast"* (verse 15). The days will come when the Bridegroom is taken away from them. I have a pastor friend who points to that passage and says, "Well, that's where the church finds itself today. Jesus is gone and that's why we fast again. Jesus said we should fast again after He left." No. The days that the Bridegroom was taken away were Friday, Saturday and Sunday morning after the crucifixion. Those were the days of mourning that Jesus talks about. Those were days when the disciples experienced lack again. They were probably so sick from grief that not a one of them ate anything. It was true fasting. The lack was so palpable that it just overcame them. They were sick with grief, sick with doubt, sick with despair, sick with fear They were grieving and longing, and weeping and tearing their clothes. But then, *resurrection*!! "Here I am!!"

Jesus is back. He breathes on them, and the Spirit of God enters into them; it's a new thing. It's not like sewing a piece of patch to our torn clothing. That's an outward solution. Our clothing is what we wear to cover our nakedness. And Jesus says that that outer garment of righteousness is torn. It's got a hole in it and our nakedness, our shame is exposed. In the Old Covenant, under the law, we would recognize that our clothing (our righteousness) has a problem. And we would beg God and plead with Him to patch up the righteousness. But even a garment that has a patch on it looks bad.

We clean up our act a bit and hope we're not exposed anywhere, but Jesus said the garment is old. *"No one puts a piece of un-shrunk cloth on an old garment"* (verse 16). The garment is old. It's full of holes. It's worn out and tattered and fragile. That's what the outer garment of your righteousness looks like. Your efforts at trying to get God to forgive, trying to cover your own shame, your own nakedness, are like patching up fragile cloth. It may cover it for a time, but it's going to keep unraveling. In fact, it's worse than that.

"No one puts a piece of un-shrunk cloth on an old garment; for the patch pulls away from the garment, and the tear is made worse." Jesus is giving them the paradigm of the New Covenant. He is saying, "This is how Old Covenant mindset people will try to relate to me in the New Covenant." You see, Jesus is the un-shrunk cloth. And this is what He says won't work — it won't work for you to hang onto the efforts of your outer righteous covering in relating to me because what you're doing is trying to take just a piece of me to use for your own purpose. Jesus is the un-shrunk cloth. When it says, "No one puts a piece of un-shrunk cloth," it literally means "no one takes an un-shrunk cloth, cuts a piece out of it, and uses that little piece to cover the hole in their garment." You can't just take a

little bit of Jesus and sew it into your old tattered righteousness robe. The tear will only get worse.

This is exactly what the church has done. This is exactly what the church has taught people to do. Step one — find the holes in your garment. Look at your sin. See where your righteousness is lacking. Look inward. Examine your life, examine your heart. Did you find the hole? Good! Step two — confess it to Jesus. "Jesus, I've got a hole in my righteousness robe, and I need a little patch of your righteousness to sew on top of it." And if you do that, if you say that and you really mean it, then you will get a little piece of Jesus; you will get a little piece of righteousness to put over your tear — but only if you mean it. You should fast just to be sure. You should cry and buffet your body and moan and weep and *be miserable*, just so you know and He knows and everyone around you knows how serious you are. Then that little patch of Jesus will be sown in good and tight. And for a while God might just say to you, "Here I am." But then He'll go away.

And we will leave God's presence (after we worked hard at getting into it), and we'll feel a little bit better, thinking that the hole is covered. But eventually, the Jesus patch pulls off. We fall again into sin and go back into the whole process again, fasting and begging and confessing. "Jesus, I'm so sorry, I need another little patch. I know I asked you before, please forgive me, just one more time." And we do that over and over and over again, until we are just worn out. And we look at the old tattered robe of our religion and we say, "It's ugly, and I can't do it anymore. It gets uglier the more I see it. I quit. I'm exhausted from sewing. I'm tired; I'm just so tired."

Jesus said that the tear is made worse. That's not New Covenant life. That's not Christianity. That's not what God intends for us. But that is the refrain that so many of us have experienced. And friend, if that's you and you're thinking, "Hey, that's sounds a little like my life with Jesus," I've got good news for you.

Jesus says, "It's not like that. Here is the description of life with me. I am new wine. And you are a new wineskin. I am not giving you a little piece of me for you to wear on the outside of your own righteousness garment; I am filling you up to the brim with myself." Here is Jesus' paradigm, His picture for the New Covenant. It involves two new things: new wine and new skins. Jesus is the new wine — powerful, fermenting, full of joy, full of life, and the old wineskin that was your efforts at righteousness can't contain him. For you to contain Jesus, He needed to remake you.

The Greeks had two different words for the word "new:" "*neos*" and "*kainos*." *Neos* has to do with a time frame. I had an old pair of tennis shoes. Now I have a new (*neos*) pair of tennis shoes. The new ones are exactly like the old ones, but they are just new in time, clean and sparkly. They are the same kind of shoes; just new in time. That's *neos. Kainos* is different. *Kainos* is new in terms of quality. It is something that didn't exist before. It is altogether uniquely new. The Bible says in 2 Corinthians 5:17 that *"those who are in Christ are new creations (kainos creations!), old things have passed away; behold, all things have become (kainos) new."*

When you became a believer in Jesus, you didn't just get your righteousness back like you had it before the fall of Adam into sin. You didn't become a *neos* creation, an updated version of the old so that now the slate is clean, but, uh-oh, what happens when I sin again? I need to get a patch for my righteousness garment to put over the hole again.

116

No! When you became a believer, Jesus made you a *kainos* creature, something completely different that never existed before. He made you something qualitatively new and perfect and righteous, something that would be so perfect and strong that it could withstand the very presence of Jesus being poured into you and filling you up to the top. Jesus is new wine, and when you became a believer in Jesus, He made you a *kainos* new-creation wineskin that cannot burst. It is made to contain Him so that you are preserved, and He poured Himself into you. He made you. He made the wineskin. You didn't make yourself a new creation — He did it, and because He did it, your wineskin is never going to leak or burst. You have the Godhead presence inside of you that does not leave.

Now this is the point. The total dynamic between you and God has changed. You can't plug the Old Testament understanding of relating to God into the reality of what Jesus has done in you. It's not you and God anymore, where the two of you are separate and you are trying to get close to Him and you are trying to get into His presence and He is up there and you are down here. Your prayers aren't making it past the ceiling and you need to somehow try harder and fast and pray and whatever.

It's not you and God with two separate existences. You are a super *kainos* wineskin, and He has totally filled you up with Himself, His spirit co-joined with your spirit and you can't get rid of Him. Jesus has totally filled you up. He has totally filled you with Himself. He has totally filled you with His righteousness. Jesus has filled you up and ferments in you. He is pushing out on every side and there is no room for anything else in you.

You are Jesus, under pressure — pressurized Jesus. That is a statement of faith. You can argue with

117

me all day long about, "Well, I have this sinful nature and I think evil thoughts and I do evil things and I envy and I get angry and I lust and, and, and." Listen, haven't we learned enough by now to base our reality on what the Word says about us and not the present flesh reality?

If I get sick, it doesn't mean that Jesus didn't purchase divine health for me. If I get sick, I don't say, "Well, I guess this is just the way it has to be." No! We take our stand with the Word of God. Jesus bore my infirmities and carried away my diseases. Same thing when we fall into sin. We don't give up on the fact that Jesus did a perfect work in me when I came to believe in Him. We take our stand on the Word of God. I have been perfected forever. *My old man was crucified with Christ and he is dead.* He's not dying. He's dead.

You are a totally new (*kainos*-new) wineskin. That is your identity. You are full up with Jesus. There is no room for anything else. You have been united with the Spirit of Jesus. There is no telling where He ends and you begin. You can't do it. Why don't you and I fast today? Because Jesus never ceases to say, "Here I am. I am right here. No striving. No fasting, no working to get clean or get God's attention. No lack!" In fact, there is now nowhere for you to run that you could get away from God.

SHEEP WITH NO SHEPHERD –
Matthew 9

Matthew chapter 9 contains five healing miracles (five miraculous, supernatural healings) that reveal to us the compassion, the love, and the healing power of Jesus. Right along with that are five teachings of Jesus that reveal the radical, revolutionary, upsetting, in your face, almost-too-good-to-be-true news of the Gospel of Jesus Christ. It was the message that religious people hated and the message that religious outcasts embraced. It was the message that God loves people, all people, and that His forgiveness is freely offered apart from your performance in holy living. God is not using your measuring rod for whether or not you are worthy of His love and forgiveness. Your Papa God uses His own measuring rod, and it is a measuring rod of grace, a measuring rod of love, and if you're a human being, you qualify. His grace is extended to you; His love is poured out on you in Jesus Christ. Right now you are forgiven of all your sins. *"For God was in Christ reconciling the world to Himself, not counting their sins against them."* God is not counting your sins against you.

> *"As they went out, behold, they brought to Him a man, mute and demon-possessed. And when the demon was cast out, the mute spoke and the multitudes marveled, saying, 'It was never seen like this in Israel!' But the Pharisees said, 'He casts out demons by the ruler of the demons.' Then Jesus went about all the cities and villages,*

teaching in their synagogues, preaching the gospel of the kingdom, and healing every sickness and every disease among the people. But when He saw the multitudes, He was moved with compassion for them, because they were weary and scattered, like sheep having no shepherd. Then He said to His disciples, 'The harvest truly is plentiful, but the laborers are few. Therefore pray the Lord of the harvest to send out laborers into His harvest.'" —Matthew 9:32-38

If you are a Gospel of Matthew fan, you know that verse 35 is part of a parenthesis that contains chapters five to nine. Matthew 4:23 says, *"And Jesus went about all Galilee teaching in their synagogues, preaching the gospel of the Kingdom, and healing all kinds of sickness and all kinds of disease among the people."* Then chapters five through nine demonstrate just that. Chapters five through seven contain Jesus' teachings on the Sermon on the Mount. Chapters eight through nine are His healings, one healing miracle after another. And it closes with the other bookend, verse 35: *"Then Jesus went about all the cities and villages, teaching in their synagogues, preaching the gospel of the kingdom, and healing every sickness and every disease among the people."*

He did that everywhere. And from that perspective (that perspective of teaching and healing all through Israel), Jesus comes up with a summary statement that tells us the spiritual condition of the Jews. *"But when He saw the multitudes, He was moved with compassion for them, because they were weary and scattered, like sheep having no shepherd"* (verse 36). My point is that this is not Jesus' reaction from seeing one particular multitude in one particular place, and that particular multitude in that particular place is having a particularly bad day. Jesus wasn't saying, "Gee, that particular crowd looks weary and scattered, like sheep without a shepherd." No. The text says "when He saw the multitudes (plural!)."

In other words, in all of the cities and all of the villages and all of the synagogues where crowds of people came and gathered day after day after day, He looked out and saw multitude after multitude, and every time He saw them He was moved with compassion for them, because every multitude (every day, in every part of Israel) was weary and scattered, like sheep having no shepherd.

Now how does Matthew the gospel writer know that is what Jesus was thinking? Obviously, Jesus shared this with His disciples and Matthew jotted it down. Jesus wants us to know why He was so moved with compassion. It was because the people were weary and scattered. That's what my Bible says; "weary and scattered." Except there's a footnote on that word "weary." If you read it you'll find that the oldest and best manuscripts don't use the word weary; they use a much more violent word *"eskulmenoi,"* which means "harassed." It's in the perfect passive tense; it means that this harassment was ongoing by some perpetrators. The multitudes are the ongoing victims to the ongoing harassment.

They were harassed and they were scattered. I want you to feel the weight of this word for *scattered.* It doesn't mean that they aren't unified, like they can't get their act together. The word is *"erimenoi"* from the root *"ripto"* which means "to throw down" or "throw away." The other place it is used is in Matthew 27:5. This is where Judas, who has just betrayed Jesus for 30 pieces of silver, goes back to the chief priests and religious rulers, and he takes the money and throws it down. To Judas, the value of that money had become worthless to him. He was throwing it away, scattering it at their feet.

Jesus applies that word to people. Jesus said in Matthew 9 that when He looked out at the multitudes He was seeing people who had been thrown away, cast aside as unimportant, without value, kicked to the curb, expendable. The verb tense is the same as the word "harassed." They were being acted upon. They were acted upon violently and had no way to defend themselves. Jesus' heart of compassion goes out to one multitude after another of people who were relentlessly being harassed and thrown away, time and time again.

But what is harassing them? What's the force that is behind this evil thing? You are going to find out because Jesus spoke it to His disciples, and then Matthew (he is all about making connections to the Old Testament) wrote it for you to see. It is the most prophetic line of this passage and if you have ears to hear, it is like an atomic explosion. It is Jesus dropping a prophetic bomb. God's people, Israel, were like sheep that had no Shepherd. That's what He says. That sounds like a rather innocuous line, except that Jesus isn't just pulling some parable out of His head. He is quoting Scripture.

Any half-way decent reference Bible is going to have a reference on that verse to Numbers 27:17 (mine does). Moses is praying here to the Lord. *"Then Moses spoke to the LORD, saying: 'Let the LORD, the God of the spirits of all flesh, set a man over the congregation, who may go out before them and go in before them, who may lead them out and bring them in, that the congregation of the LORD may not be like sheep which have no shepherd'"* (Numbers 27:15-17). This is the only place in all of Scripture where that exact language is used to describe God's people Israel. Jesus is making a direct connect for you. You were supposed to make this direct connect.

What is Jesus pointing to? I'll give you the context. Moses was leading the people. They have been 40 years out in the wilderness and now they are at the edge of the Promised Land. But Moses is not allowed to lead the people into the Promised Land. Why? This is God talking in verse 14: *"For in the wilderness of Zin, during the strife of the congregation, you rebelled against my command to hallow me at the waters before their eyes."* God is reminding Moses of the incident that happened at Zin. The people grumbled and needed water. God told Moses to take the rod of Aaron and go before the rock and speak to the rock, and waters would gush out for the people. But Moses went up to the rock (this is Numbers 20:10-11): *"And Moses and Aaron gathered the assembly together before the rock; and he said to them, 'Hear now, you rebels! Must we bring water for you out of this rock?' Then Moses lifted his hand and struck the rock twice with his rod and water came out abundantly, and the congregation and their animals drank."*

God got very upset about that and told Moses that he could not enter the Promised Land because *"you did not believe me, to hallow me in the eyes of the children of Israel, therefore you shall not bring this assembly into the land which I have given you"* (verse 12). I used to read this and say, "What!? Come on, God. Moses led your people for 40 years in the wilderness, gave his whole life to lead them to the Promised Land and now, because one time he hits the rock instead of speaks to the rock, you take away the Promised Land from him?!" Does that seem fair to you? Is God over-reacting here just a little bit?! Have you ever thought that?

No, God isn't over-reacting. Here's what was happening. God was painting a picture (a masterpiece) of redemption in Jesus (in typology) and Moses stole the paint brush. There were actually two times that water was brought out of the rock. The first time happened at the beginning of their wanderings in the wilderness where God's people didn't have any water, just like in this instance. God tells Moses in Exodus 17:5-6: *"Go on before the people and take with you some of the elders of Israel. Also take in your hand your rod with which you struck the river, and go. Behold, I will stand before you there on the rock in Horeb, and you shall strike the rock and water will come out of it that the people may drink."* And Moses did so in the sight of the Elders of Israel. Moses struck the rock, and water came out. Nice miracle. But it's not just a miracle. It's a picture. The Bible says in 1 Corinthians 10:4, referring to this miracle: *"And they (Israel) drank the same spiritual drink; for they drank from the spiritual rock that accompanied them, and that rock was Christ."* Paul says that the rock from which Israel drank was Jesus.

What's going on in this miracle/picture that Papa God is painting? Jesus, *before the elders*, is being struck down. The rod of judgment is coming against Him. Moses is carrying the rod of judgment, *"the rod with which you struck the river"* (verse 5). This is the rod of judgment that turned the waters of the Nile into blood. Water became blood. Water becomes judgment. This was the plague upon Egypt. (Interesting that Jesus' first miracle is to turn water into wine, water into the sign of the New Covenant, water into blessing. Jesus undoes the curse of judgment).

But in the first water miracle, Moses is instructed to strike the rock with the rod of judgment. Who is there? The Elders of Israel. Who is responsible for the striking down of Jesus? The Elders of Israel. It's a picture! Jesus takes the judgment rod upon Himself. And as soon as He takes the judgment rod upon Himself, things change. There is a new way to receive blessing. That is part one of the picture.

Now, 40 years later they come to the wilderness of Zin. The people are thirsty and God is going to finish painting the picture. The people are grumbling, *but God does not get angry with them.* You would think that God would be mad. He's not mad. They sin; He doesn't get mad. God wants to meet their need. He wants to bless them. He's not responding like you expect. That's kind of weird, which remember, that's really the bottom line definition of holy. Holy means "other," holy means "different." God is holy because He does not act and react the way we think He should.

God says to Moses, "Go to the rock." Who is the rock? It's Jesus. "But this time, don't take your rod of judgment. Take Aaron's rod, the rod that just miraculously bloomed in a single night." You read this in chapter 17, where this rod put forth buds and put forth blossoms and produced almonds. It was a sign of the resurrection. Take the resurrection rod and go up to the rock, and speak to the rock. And it will pour forth water. It was the new way of receiving from God. With resurrection power in your hand, you speak out your need. You speak to Jesus. *"Moses, speak to the rock."*

And Moses did not speak to the rock. He thought it was all the same and nothing had changed. He walked up to the rock and he hurled insults and condemnation at God's people, and he struck the rock with the resurrection rod, treating it just like a judgment rod. He was treating the rock (Jesus) just like He had not taken the judgment, just like nothing had changed. (That sounds like some preachers I know personally, mixing judgment and grace.) That's what got God mad! We're not to do that. Moses did not understand the painting. Moses thought blessings should flow with condemnations. ("People need to be humbled. People need to know their sin.")

God said, "No! Moses! You have misrepresented me. *You rebelled against my command* (Moses is the rebel — not the people!) *to hallow me at the waters before their eyes"* (Chapter 27, Verse 14). You didn't make me appear weird to the people. You made me appear like the God who is mad at them because you think I should be mad at them. But I'm not. I just want to bless them! I am not holding their complaining against them. And I am not going to let you lead them into the Promised Land, because I'm not going to have my people think that your picture is the right picture. I'm not going to have your picture presented, which is: "You only get blessing by admitting your sin. You only get blessing with condemnation. You only get blessing when you mix condemnation of the law and grace. No, that is not me."

It's a rebuke. God rebukes Moses. But that rebuke was for your sake so you wouldn't get the wrong idea, because God loved Moses. Papa puts this prophetic word in Moses' mouth as a prayer: *"Let the Lord, the God of the spirits of all flesh, set a man over the congregation who may go out before them, and go in before them, who may lead them out and bring them in that the congregation of the Lord may not be like sheep which have no shepherd"* (verses 16-17). Who is the man that God is going to set over His people so that they *will* have a shepherd? It's Jesus!

Moses, the law bringer, Moses the condemnation speaker, could not lead God's people into the Promised Land. The Promised Land, to the believer, is a symbol. Read about it in Hebrews 4. The Promised Land for you represents all of the blessings that God has for you,

His people. It's everything He provides for us — salvation, protection, righteousness, peace, love, comfort, healing, food, clothing, job, security. God gives it to us.

But the point is this: *the law cannot lead you into the Promised Land.* You don't get miracle rescue, miracle help, miracle righteousness, miracle comfort by being good and trying to appease God. The law and its judgment can only harass you. The law and its ensuing judgment only makes you feel worthless, as someone that is not worth saving and redeeming. Your guilt under the law makes you feel valueless, as someone that is fit only to be tossed away. No! Jesus looked out on the multitudes and He saw them harassed and tossed aside. Why? They were living without a shepherd, a shepherd who would protect them from the harassing/belittling power of the law. They needed Jesus to be that Shepherd.

What does Moses say that this Shepherd will do? *"He will go out before them, and go in before them, who may lead them out and bring them in"* (verse 17). What is this "going out and going in?" Think about this; where are Moses and the people right now in this story? They are in the wilderness. This Shepherd, first of all, blazes the trail from out of the wilderness into the Promised Land. He will *"Go out before them* (out of the wilderness) *and He will go in before them* (into the Promised Land)." That is what Jesus did in His death and resurrection. He went from us and went into the place of blessing and abundance, at the right hand of God. And then, after He blazes the trail, He comes back for them. He will *"lead them out and bring them in."*

Listen, brother. Listen, sister. *He does not leave you in the wilderness. He has come back for you.* Jesus has taken the rod of judgment onto Himself. God is not angry with you, ever. He just wants to bless you. Jesus, the new Shepherd blazed the trail out of the wilderness and into the Promised Land. And He has come back to the camp; He has come back to you so that you will not be stuck in the wilderness. There are a lot of people stuck in the wilderness, and they think the law (and doing right) is going to get them out.

He is leading you out of it and bringing you to a new place, He is leading you to His Promised Land where God takes care of you and you know His love and you are finally, finally able to rest and relax in His care. You are not like sheep without a shepherd.

THE BAPTISM OF JESUS

There is a lot of confusion about what baptism is and what it isn't, why we do it and should we do it, and do we have to do it, and how do we do it. And "your sprinkling doesn't count" and "your immersion doesn't count because it wasn't done in our church, so you're still going to hell." And "baptism *only* counts for babies, until they make shipwreck of their baptism" and, "no, baptism is *never* meant for babies because they can't decide." This is fighting territory among the Pharisees, so I am absolutely sure I'm going to step on lots of toes. But if you can receive this and let me open the Scriptures to you, you will find the joy and beauty of baptism.

Baptism is not a requirement for salvation; it is a gift from Jesus to empower you. The thief on the cross was not baptized, but he entered into paradise with Jesus. The Gentile converts that Peter visited were filled with the Holy Spirit as they heard the gospel. In other words, they were redeemed without baptism. But the very next thing Peter did was water baptize because of the power inherent in the gift. Jesus told His disciples to preach the gospel, demonstrate the power of the kingdom with miracles, and baptize in the name of the Father, the Son, and Holy Spirit.

There are two gifts that Jesus gave to His bride: communion and baptism. To say, "Oh, I don't need to be baptized," is the same thing as saying, "I don't need to receive Holy Communion." That's true. You can reject every beautiful gift that Jesus wants to give you and, if you have faith in Him, you will be with Him in heaven. You will just be missing out on the means to blessings, because communion and baptism are

Christ's gifts to you to strengthen your faith and provide you with a visible, material point of contact for your faith. They are unduplicated on the earth by anything else you could conjure up. Jesus thought it was important for you to have this gift. And as you understand it, you will see the power of it in your life.

Jesus' baptism was a transitional baptism. He transitioned humanity from John's baptism to the new baptism of the Spirit. *"Then Jesus came from Galilee to John at the Jordan to be baptized by him. And John tried to prevent Him, saying, 'I need to be baptized by you, and are you coming to me?' But Jesus answered and said to him, 'Permit it to be so now, for thus it is fitting for us to fulfill all righteousness.' Then he allowed Him. When He had been baptized, Jesus came up immediately from the water and behold, the heavens were opened to Him, and He saw the Spirit of God descending like a dove and alighting upon Him. And suddenly a voice came from heaven, saying, 'This is my beloved Son, in whom I am well pleased'"* (Matthew 3:13-17).

Jesus came to John the Baptist to be baptized. Think about this. Jesus was baptized into John's baptism. John was the last Old Testament prophet. The Old Testament prophet's job was to call people back to the law. Their job was to point out all your mistakes and all your sins and get you to try harder at being good. St. Paul (in the New Testament) says that this Old Covenant of the law was given so that every mouth may be stopped. The system was given to show that we need a savior who will rescue us from our sin because the Jews were in this perpetual cycle of breaking the law, entering into sin, getting themselves cleansed from sin and getting right with God, then breaking the law and entering sin, and doing that over and over again.

Within the system itself were constant reminders that you were not measuring up. One of those reminders of sin was the washings that the Jews would do throughout the day to get uncleanness off. You would wash three times before eating, not to get rid of dirt, but to get rid of sin, to get rid of spiritual uncleanness. Priests would wash before they would sacrifice. The High Priest would wash before Atonement. A scribe, before he could write the name of God, had to wash. Regular worshippers would wash. Converts to Judaism would wash.

There were many occasions to wash. Men and women would wash before entering into the temple. In fact, archeology has uncovered 47 baths (like big tubs that would hold 200 gallons of water — they were called "*mikveh*") all around the Temple for men and women to wash. Why? Because they were spiritually dirty. It was an admittance of sin, a confession of uncleanness. The *mikveh* was the place of washing where you were making a public statement that said, "I am a sinner, and I need to be cleaned. I need the mercy of God before I am acceptable." And one of the things that you would say as you were coming out of the water was profess your allegiance to the Torah, the law of God, and you would say, "I will do and I will hear." I will do better, and I put myself back under the law and the cycle of sin, repent, confess, get clean perpetuates itself.

This was the baptism of John. The baptism of John was a public confession that you are a sinner, and unclean, and in getting baptized you were saying, "God clean me and I promise to do better. I turn my back on my sin; I repent of my sin." Look at Matthew 3:5-6: *"Then Jerusalem, Judea, and all the region around the Jordan went out to him (John) and were baptized by him in the Jordan, confessing their sins."* That was the baptism that Jesus was baptized into — the baptism of repentance, changing your mind about your sin, and confessing your sin and your need for forgiveness. Jesus was baptized into that.

That is why John protested when Jesus the Messiah came to him to be baptized. John recognized that it wasn't right that sinless Jesus, the Messiah, confess sin, repent of sin, and cry out for mercy. There is no logic to it. Why do this? Jesus said, *"Permit it to be so now, for thus it is fitting for us to fulfill all righteousness"* (verse 15). We're doing this, John, to fulfill righteousness. In other words, righteousness is lacking and this is part of what needs done to fulfill righteousness. Well, righteousness was already full up in Jesus. Jesus was righteous. So whose righteousness is lacking that needs fulfilled? Yours! Your righteousness is lacking and needs fulfilled. What is Jesus doing? Jesus is taking your place, being baptized for you into the baptism of confession and repentance of sin, and He is the only person who came up out of the waters able to fulfill the repentance saying, "I will do, I will hear." Jesus took your sin upon himself at His baptism and carried them for 3 years! What a beautiful thought. This is why he could say to the lame man, "your sins *are* forgiven you" and not "your sins *will be* forgiven you." Hallelujah!

Just as Jesus took your place in payment for your sins so that you never have to pay for any of your sins, Jesus also took your place in repentance and confession of your sin, so that you never have to do that again. When you were under the law and confessing sin all the time, didn't you always wonder, "Well, I wonder if I repented good enough. I wonder if I got all my sins confessed. I wonder if I dug deep enough into my psyche in finding the root of the sins; I wonder if I could have repented better." Yes, of course you could have. Jesus set you free from this. Freedom! This was step one in fulfilling all righteousness for you. And as soon as Jesus stepped out of the waters of confession and repentance, the baptism of John became spiritually dead. It was no longer necessary. Jesus was introducing a new baptism.

John the Baptist knew that this would happen. He says, *"I indeed baptize you with water unto repentance, but He who is coming after me is mightier than I, whose sandals I am not worthy to carry. He will baptize you with the Holy Spirit and fire"* (verse 11). Jesus will introduce a new baptism. It will not be a baptism of confession and repentance of sin. It will be a baptism of the Holy Spirit and fire. I think this is one of the most misunderstood phrases of the New Testament. The baptism into which you are baptized as a believer is a baptism of the Holy Spirit (which is God's permanent presence on you and in you) and fire. The "fire" here is what throws people. But there is no getting around this.

The fire is the judgment of God upon you. God judges you in baptism. You know, we have been trained to fear the judgment of God. When we think of the judgment of God, we have been conditioned by the church to think "the *condemnation* of God." But judgment is simply the pronouncement of a decision. God is the judge and He makes judgments, positive or negative. What is the judgment of God that Jesus brings to you in your baptism? I will show you. I could show you from the New Testament, but I want you to see the beauty of Jesus in the Old Testament as well. The good teacher brings out revelations old and new. The Old Testament is entirely about Jesus. Someone once said, "Take a pin and prick any verse of any chapter of any book in the Old Testament and it will bleed the blood of Christ."

But there are "crescendos" in the Old Testament where Jesus is seen so clearly. One of those places is the instructions for the building of the Temple, and especially, the design of the vestments for the High Priest. Jesus is our High Priest and He is clearly seen in the vestments. In Exodus, chapter 28, it talks about the breastplate of the High Priest and calls it "the breastplate of judgment." In other words, this is worn over the heart of the High Priest, the place of faith, and it represents the judgment of God. And there are many special things that point to Jesus in the breastplate of judgment, but the greatest of them all is in verse 30: *"And you shall put in the breastplate of judgment the Urim and the Thummim, and they shall be over Aaron's heart when he goes in before the Lord, so Aaron shall bear the judgment of the children of Israel over his heart before the Lord continually."*

The fact is that nobody really knows what the Urim and Thummim are that they fixed into the breastplate of judgment. What did they look like? Nobody really knows. I think God wanted it that way. Because the power and presence of Jesus are clearly seen without some picture of what the objects were. This is a picture of Jesus. The "im" ending in the Hebrew is a plural ending such as Seraph (one angel); seraphim (more than one angel). The Urim and Thummim are plural, but they are not plural. The context in the Hebrew suggests that this is *pluralis intensivus* — they are singular words that are pluralized to enhance their majesty. In other words, there is something divine going on here.

If you get out your Hebrew Bible (or, if you have an Aleph Tav Old Testament), you would see the Aleph Tav (the signature of Jesus, the Alpha and Omega) here. The actual verse reads, *"And you shall put in the breastplate of Judgment the Aleph-Tav Urim*

134

and Thummim, and they shall be over Aaron's heart." What goes over Aaron's heart? What is the judgment of God that Aaron is to wear all the time? The judgment that Jesus renders over him. What is that? Urim means "light" or "flame." It is translated many times as "fire" in the Old Testament. Thummim means "innocence." What is the judgment that Jesus brings? *Jesus brings the judgment, the fire of innocence over us.*

You, oh believer, <u>want</u> the judgment of God on your life because it is the pronouncement of your innocence in Jesus. When you are sick, you should cry out to God for judgment. "Judge me, oh Lord, for the fiery innocence of your Son is on me. Declare this sickness unjust upon me. Judge me, oh Lord." That is part of the new baptism that Jesus brings. It is a baptism of fire. And brothers, and sisters, it is an all-consuming fire. It burns up everything that is not of faith in Christ. It burns up everything in your life that is born of your own efforts in relating to God under the law, trying to please God, trying to maintain your relationship with God, thinking that you are the one that keeps yourself clean and gets yourself clean. No, you must let the fire burn that up.

John the Baptist said of Jesus (verses 11-12): *"He will baptize you with the Holy Spirit and with fire.* Now listen to the fire part; *"His winnowing fan is in His hand, and He will thoroughly clean out His threshing floor and gather His wheat into the barn, but He will burn the chaff with unquenchable fire."* The fire is the judgment Jesus brings (to what?!) to the chaff.

I am by no means a farmer, but I know this; that if you raise wheat, the first thing that a stalk produces is the chaff. It's the shell that forms, and then within the shell the grains of wheat appear. It's the grains of wheat that you want. In the stalk of Israel, the first thing that appeared was the law (a system of relating to

135

God based on your doing and your maintaining the relationship — and if you lived holy then you were blessed and if you failed at living holy, you were cursed). But what was emerging in front of John the Baptist right now? The wheat was forming, the wheat of the good news of Jesus. It was the good news of grace where Jesus establishes a New Covenant based on His goodness and His righteousness and His payment for sin so that you will be blessed apart from your performance in holiness.

You partake by believing. You believe that Jesus did this for you. You believe that you are blessed in Christ. You believe that the Urim and Thummim are upon your breast and the fiery judgment of Christ's innocence is worn over you 24/7. It is your badge and your reward. God judges you innocent. God says of you, just like He says of His Son, "You are my beloved son, in whom I am well pleased." That is true as soon as you believe it.

Everything that is apart from that, everything apart from Christ's work, is burned up as chaff. Every area of your life where you relate to God based on your doing is worthless and will be burned up. The Christian life is not about your doing. It is Holy Spirit and fire. It is living out of God who is alive in you, and letting Jesus burn everything else; everything that comes out of the law and what you are doing to please God.

That is why we do not baptize into John's baptism. What does your baptism into Christ mean? Into what are you baptized? St. Paul says in Romans 6:3-4: *"Or do you not know that as many of us as were baptized into Christ Jesus were baptized into His death? Therefore we were buried with Him through baptism into death, that just as Christ was raised from the dead by the glory of the Father, even so we also should walk in newness of life."* Buried with Jesus, and raised with Jesus. Believer's water baptism is a personal and public statement that you are trusting only in the finished work of redemption that Jesus accomplished for you.

I died with Jesus, and I am raised up with Jesus to a new way of living. And it has nothing to do with my efforts and confessing sin, repenting of sin, maintaining my relationship with God through my redoubled efforts at living pure. No. We spit on that. We repudiate everything that comes out of our own strength. That is filthy rags. My relationship with God is not based anymore on my doing. It is based on my living out of God who lives in me. I ask God what He wants. He tells me. He puts desires in my heart. I don't even think in terms of right or wrong or sin or righteousness. The Spirit is in me and leading me, and I live a miracle life of blessing and joy.

When we are baptized into Christ's death and resurrection, we are saying, "It's not even me who lives anymore, but Christ who lives in me. I live out of God. I don't try to please God. I am pleasing already to Him. I don't try to become righteous. I am the righteousness of God in Christ." And the only agenda item on my life plan is to "live out of the God that inhabits me."

That is the exact opposite of saying, "I'm going down to the river to show God that I've changed my life. And now that I know Jesus, I am going to redouble my efforts at holy living, and I'm going to confess my sin, and repent and try real hard to do better and please my Father in heaven." No!! That is the baptism of John, the whole "I'm getting a new suit for my baptism and I don't want to get it dirty with my sin. I want to honor my new suit." No! Chaff! Stubble! Let the fire of Jesus' work burn it up.

Here is my contention. I don't care what words were spoken at the time of their baptism; most believers were baptized into the baptism of John, which was a baptism of confession and repentance of sin. And they came out the other end with no power to live righteously or victoriously because the baptism of John is just your efforts. If you were baptized into Christ, you should despise that. You should see that for the mockery and filthy rags that it is.

One time, St. Paul stumbled upon some believers in Jesus who had no power for living and he immediately diagnosed the problem. This is Acts 19:3-6: *"And he said to them, 'Into what then were you baptized?' So they said, 'Into John's baptism.' Then Paul said, 'John indeed baptized with a baptism of repentance, saying to the people that they should believe on Him who would come after him, that is, on Christ Jesus.' When they heard this, they were baptized in the name of the Lord Jesus. And when Paul had laid hands on them, the Holy Spirit came upon them, and they spoke with tongues and prophesied.'"*

John's baptism was a baptism of human effort. We are baptized in Jesus' baptism. Think about this: Jesus' baptism was not the baptism in the Jordan that John performed that day. His baptism was His death and resurrection that would bring the fire judgment of God. He says in Luke 12:49-50, *"I came to send fire* (what fire? the fire that burns up the chaff of human effort and pronounces your innocence) *on the earth, and how I wish it were already kindled! But I have a baptism to be baptized with, and how distressed I am till it is accomplished!"* Now that's His death. When you are baptized into Christ, you are baptized into His own baptism which is the death of who you were before God as a sinner, and the resurrection to a new creation in Christ, never to be judged by God as a sinner again — ever. And your baptism becomes the substantive moment of faith that you can point to that says, "That's who I am."

Under the Old Covenant, you could not be baptized without a witness present. That way, if there was ever a dispute, the witness could step in and say, "Hey, I was there. This really happened. I vouch for this person." Scholars believe that this is where the phrase being baptized "in the name of" a person arose. When we baptize a person into Christ, the Lord says that we are baptizing them "in the name of the Father and the Son and the Holy Spirit." The entire Godhead becomes your witness. They vouch for you. "This one belongs to me forever." God attends your baptism as your witness, as your Godfather.

The fiery judgment of Jesus is seen in the story of Shadrach, Meshach, and Abednego. If you can receive it, this is a story of fire baptism. The three Hebrew men are thrown into the furnace because they broke the law and the fire is made seven times hotter than usual. But Jesus shows up and the fire becomes His fire and it becomes a picture of His deliverance. And the only things burned up on the Hebrew sons are the bindings on their legs and hands. Make your home in the fiery innocence of Jesus.

VOICE OF THE SHEPHERD – John 10

"Most assuredly, I say to you, he who does not enter the sheepfold by the door, but climbs up some other way, the same is a thief and a robber. But he who enters by the door is the shepherd of the sheep. To him the doorkeeper opens, and the sheep hear his voice; and he calls his own sheep by name and leads them out. And when he brings out his own sheep, he goes before them; and the sheep follow him, for they know his voice; yet they will by no means follow a stranger, but will flee from him, for they do not know the voice of strangers." — John 10:1-5

Jesus told this parable of the sheep and how the sheep hear the shepherd's voice and follow him., There are really so many encouraging things here. Notice Jesus begins with the words, "Most assuredly." This is Jesus' way of saying "listen up!" It's really, in the Greek, "Amen, amen." And "amen" is not even a Greek word; it's a Hebrew word that means "certainty," or "surely." Jesus is saying, "Absolutely true, absolutely true!" Like, "Get your pads and pens out, you will want to write this down."

In the previous verse, Jesus is having a run-in with the Pharisees over healing the man who was blind from birth. There was a whole crowd of people with Jesus, and not all of them were His followers. "Then some of the Pharisees who were with Him (Pharisees who were traveling with Him) heard these words and said to Him, *'Are we blind also?' Jesus said to them, 'If you were blind you would have no sin, but now you say "we see;" therefore your sin remains'* (John 9:40-41).

This is comparing the two approaches, the two covenants, the two systems of living. The Law approach of the Pharisees is that we will be good enough for God by our efforts. They love this way. They are teachers of this way. They say, "We see the way to God, and it is through rigorous holy living." And Jesus tells them that because they say "we see," their sin remains. You are unforgiven and you are still blind. The other way is the way of freely receiving God's forgiveness, love, and acceptance in Jesus.

Jesus just had this run-in with the Pharisees, and then says, *"Most assuredly* (write this down, write this down; surely, surely; pay attention to this); *he who does not enter the sheepfold by the door, but climbs up some other way, the same is a thief and a robber."* Who is He talking about? The Pharisees as teachers, those who wish to gain access to the sheep. Where are the sheep? They are penned in — in an enclosure. They are walled in on all sides. Are you seeing the Law Covenant here? The Pharisees want to be teachers to the sheep. They want theological access to the sheep. They attempt to climb up over the wall that pens the sheep in, by their own strength, in order to steal the sheep. They are rejecting the door because the door is Jesus. Jesus says a little later, "I am the door."

Jesus Himself made the opening into the sheep pen (into the law system that penned us in). He has become the door. And then He says, "I am the shepherd. I am the door, and I am the shepherd." And as the shepherd, He goes into the sheep pen and leads the sheep out of there. Notice He does not go in to be with the sheep in their enclosure (and make a home with them in the enclosure). He goes in to get them out. *"He calls His own sheep by name and leads them out. And when He brings out His own sheep, He goes before them and the sheep follow Him, for they know His voice"* (verses 3-4).

So He gets the sheep out of the enclosure. Then what? How do the sheep live their lives? They live their lives by the personal voice of the shepherd (that they are following), and not the impersonal walls and parameters of the law. We exchange the impersonal stone tablets of the Old Covenant for the personal voice of Jesus. And this is really where the grace message gets exciting because the grace message of Jesus is not just a doctrine like some other doctrine. It is not just a theology or philosophy of life, something that's a little easier to follow. No, the Gospel message is fellowship with God, and hearing the voice of Jesus.

If Grace is just a doctrine, just an understanding between you and God, you've really missed it. Grace isn't just — "God is not angry with me when I do something wrong." Grace is so much greater than just God forgiving me. Grace is access to direct fellowship with God. In Jesus, you are reborn of God, born again in the spirit. And we have not been born again to be set free into doing wrong things and not feeling badly about it. But in grace, we have been set free from the power of sin and death to participate in abundant life. I am not set free so that I can do drugs and still know that Jesus loves me (that is true). But we have been set free to experience God and the resurrection power of Jesus in order to have no addictions to anything, in order to find healing and in order to experience joy and the fullness of life with God and with loved ones and with God's children. We are set free *from* death and *from* things that destroy us in order to be set free *into* life with Jesus and good works, the very manifestation of God in our lives. We get to hear from God, as much as we want.

This is something extraordinary that has happened in us, something Old Covenant people couldn't imagine. You hear the voice of God! You hear the voice of Jesus! In the Old Testament, you couldn't hear God's voice. Under that covenant, God would speak to one man and then that man would communicate God's message to the rest of the people. Under Grace, you yourself hear the voice of the Shepherd. You have heard His voice. You have! Jesus says, *"And the sheep hear his voice; and he calls his own sheep by name and leads them out"* (verse 3).

Now this is very important. How do you hear the voice of Jesus? Jesus' own voice came to you in the words of His Gospel of Grace. You heard His voice and He led you out of the law. You responded to His Gospel of Grace and as you believed it, you came to realize that He was calling you individually. "He calls His own by name." This is just how He is. There is no blanket doctrine of grace that circumvents human will. That's why there isn't a universalism, where God just trumps human will and forces everyone to go to heaven.

God loves you as a sovereign being, and He calls you by name. Think about this. Jesus called you by name. Jesus uses your name. Everyone knows the intimacy of this. There is nothing in the world like hearing the sound of your name on the lips of a person who loves you. My wife can call me "Baby" or "sweetheart" or (you don't even want to know the names she calls me). But still, after all these years, there is nothing that compares to her speaking my name to me. "Greg, would you put the coffee on?" That is a powerful thing, because your name is the very symbol of your identity. When you hear your name, you know that it means everything you are, everything you ever have been, and everything you will ever become. When you hear your name spoken, you know that everything that's about to follow, applies specifically for you. How powerful and intimate when it comes from the lips of a person who loves you!

When Jesus came to you in the sheep pen, at the time of your life when you were scarred and bruised from bumping into the walls of the Law Covenant, Jesus Himself (right here in this passage) said that He called your name. "Bill, I have come for you. Suzanne, I am not holding anything against you. John, hear me; I am never mad at you. Lori, you are not unlovable; I love you. Peter, Peter, let's get out of here; I'm the door. Angela, wake up, you are in Papa's family. You are His precious daughter forever and ever. It will not end."

Jesus said He used your name, and what did He do? He personally applied the word of grace, and you knew it was for you. The word of grace was for you. His voice came in the word of grace. And you believed it, and Jesus brought you out. You heard His voice. It wasn't an audible voice. It was an intuitive voice that came with the word of grace. In other words, His voice sounded exactly like the word of grace. And the word of grace, as you received it by name, caused you to desire certain things. "I want to give my life to Jesus. I want Him to rescue me. I enjoy experiencing God's love. I love Him back. I want to listen to this teaching on grace. I want to read this book on God's love." What is happening is that these desires in you are the voice of Jesus that has come through the word of grace. That's how you started hearing it.

How do you keep hearing the voice of Jesus? Keep abiding in the word of grace. Jesus said, *"Abide in my word."* You keep feeding on the word of grace and as you feed on the word of grace, things will pop into your mind and heart and what you are hearing (at that point) is the voice of Jesus personally speaking to you. Now this is the most exciting thing to me. But it does come with a caveat, and that is that if you are not abiding in His word, (in other words, if you allow your mind to find its home in fears or insecurities or wounded-ness) what you hear will not be the voice of God because your believing is fixed on something other than Jesus.

And this is the axiom: *a person can only hear what they believe*. I'll tell you what I mean. If you want to get freaked out, Google "the voice of God" and see what you find. I took about an hour recently to read web pages and listen to videos of people who were talking about Jesus' voice. Let me tell you, weirdness abounds. People are hearing what they believe.

I listened to one man go on and on about how many believers in Jesus, people who have faith in Him, are going to hell. And the determining factor of a believer in Jesus going to hell or not, according to this man, was whether or not they could audibly hear the voice of Jesus. He was preaching from this passage in John 10. "If you don't audibly hear the voice of Jesus," he said, "You may believe, but you are not His sheep." Hey, that is wrong! How do I know it's wrong? That message would never arise from the platform of grace. He is hearing condemnation. He is hearing what he believes.

I'll tell you something wonderful. We have something so much better than the audible voice of God. We have a much higher form of communication with Papa than audible words, something much more powerful and louder than external words. If you were a father, and you had a choice of either speaking to your son by an audible voice or by plopping your very desires into the heart of your son so that your desires actually became his desires, which one would you do? Which one of those is the higher form of communication? Is it an audible external word or an internal desire in the heart? Man, this is how intimate and powerfully God makes His voice heard to us now. And it is easy to recognize the voice of God, the voice of Jesus Himself. It comes with the word of grace.

The thing that anchors us is the words of Jesus, the words that delivered us from the sheep pen, the words of grace. *That's what His voice sounds like.* His voice will always come in those words, surrounded by those words, in the midst of the words of your new identity. You are righteous. You are His son. You are in Papa's grip. No one can snatch you out of His hand. You are a new creature in Him. You are joined with Christ. He is your shepherd. You are taken care of. All your needs are met.

As you meditate (as you abide) in His word of grace, the things that will come up out of your mind and out of your heart will be desires that are born of God. But if you do not abide in His word (abiding in what He says about you), you will find that the things that rise up in you are born out of fears or condemnations or hurts or wounded parts of your soul. Not everything you think and feel is the voice of Jesus. Jesus does not want to thump the person ahead of you on 71st street outside of the mall because they are such a stupid driver. ("Get 'em, Jesus! Shall I call down fire from heaven!") *You* want to do that because that idea in you is *born out of frustration.* Do you see what I mean? That is not the voice of Jesus. I guarantee it.

The voice of Jesus comes to you out of your place of contentment in the word of grace. The Bible says in Psalm 37:4, *"Delight yourself in the Lord, and He shall give you the desires of your heart."* I used to think that this meant that we have to work hard at praising God, work hard at delighting in His presence. And when I get to that place where I have delighted in God enough and God is satisfied with my delightedness in Him, (the delightfulness meter in heaven reads "full") then God will give me the new car I want or the new job I need or give you the boyfriend you've been asking for. Delighting in the Lord was the key to getting your favorite Christmas present from God.

But that's all backwards. *Delighting yourself in the Lord is finding the delight God has over you.* It's the Old Testament equivalent of Jesus saying, "Abide in my word. Remember who you are to me (that's nothing but good news; you find delight there); you are my son and I love you; here's what I have done for you. I've got everything taken care of for you." It is coming to that place of contentment in God and His love, because you know how loved you are by Him. It is partaking of His goodness for you. That is delighting yourself in the Lord. In fact, that word for "delighting" is literally translated as *"enjoying the deliciousness of the Lord."* If you were to study this out, it has an effeminate connotation to it, the idea of softness and luxuriousness is behind it. It's like for you ladies, going to a resort or a spa and getting the mud treatment or the massage treatment. *It is luxuriating in the pampering of God.*

The gospel of God is that *He wants to do for you.* The gospel is "God does for us." The Law Covenant is "you do for God," where you become the servant/slave. But Jesus said the greatest in the kingdom is servant of all. Jesus is the greatest in the kingdom, and He came to be servant of all. If you insist on being the servant of Jesus, you have put yourself in the position of lordship over Him.

You are not here to be the servant of the Lord. God desires to serve you. He desires to wash your feet. And if that is upsetting to you (like it was to Peter at the last supper) then you have no part in Him. What that means is that you cannot find the benefit of being in Christ if you are not allowing Jesus to serve you. God wants you to luxuriate in Him. He wants to pamper you. And when you enter into that place of pampering, where you are abiding in the words of goodness and life of Jesus, you will find (in that place, in that gracious place of your identity) certain desires arising from within you. Those desires are born of God and are the voice of God. They are born of God precisely because they rise from the word of grace and not from your wounded-ness or your neediness or your hurt or your condemnation or your guilt. You know you are hearing God when you delight yourself in the Lord, because that is when He puts into you the desires of your heart.

Jesus said, *"My sheep hear my voice; I call them by name. I bring them out of their enclosure, and they follow me, for they know my voice."* Jesus speaks to you in the word of grace, you follow Him out of the enclosure, and now real life begins. He continues to speak to you, you follow Him, and you know His voice. Sheep don't listen to the voice of a stranger.

The thief is the one who comes to take that away from you. "The thief does not come except to steal and to kill and to destroy. I have come that they may have life and that they may have it abundantly" (verse 10). A thief comes in order to steal what rightly belongs to you. A thief will say that you are not able to hear Jesus' voice. A thief will say, "Only I can; you should listen to me. I can hear better." What have they done? They have stolen your confidence that Jesus speaks to you. A thief will say you are lacking before God in some way, that you need to get yourself right before God (stealing your confidence). A thief will say you need the law of God to hear from God. No, you only need to know who you are in Christ, His Spirit in you.

148

Don't listen to the thief because Jesus said now that you understand His grace, you will not hear the voice of a stranger. You will only hear Jesus' voice.

Satan comes with many other voices to steal, kill, and destroy. And any other voice besides the word of grace in Jesus will be a voice that has come to steal, kill, and destroy. It will steal your inheritance. "Oh, God, I am not good enough to deserve your blessings. I am a failure; I failed my family, I failed my children, I failed my spouse; I am not qualified." The devil wants to kill the good image of you that is truly who you are in Jesus. He can't really mar who you are; just distort your self-image, to mar it, destroy it, and keep you faithless.

Why is it so hard for some people to believe that Jesus wants to give abundant life? The devil steals, kills, and destroys. He does exactly the opposite of Jesus. Jesus does the opposite of the devil. He doesn't steal; taking from you what doesn't belong to Him. He does the opposite; He gifts you with things that belong to Him and He gives them to you. He doesn't kill you; He resurrects you to a new life. He doesn't mar your self-image to destroy you; He speaks of how beautiful you are. You are beautiful to Jesus. He sees you lovely. That is the Song of Solomon, the love song of Jesus over you. He sees you beautiful.

Abide in those words. Delight yourself in His good opinion over you. That is where you find abundant life. And that is where God communicates with you on a level far greater than audible words. He shares His mind and heart with you. Believe this. Jesus called you by name and He still calls you by name. Jesus led you out by the word of grace, your new identity, and He still leads you. Jesus spoke to you by the word of grace and He still speaks to you. You hear His voice. You are His sheep. See the intimacy of that.

Hear His voice. What are the things rising up in you right now? That's Him. What are you feeling toward people in your life? What are the things you want to do? *That is His voice.*

REVELATION
THE CHURCH AT EPHESUS

"The mystery of the seven stars which you saw in My right hand, and the seven golden lampstands: The seven stars are the angels of the seven churches, and the seven lampstands which you saw are the seven churches. "To the angel of the church of Ephesus write, 'These things says He who holds the seven stars in His right hand, who walks in the midst of the seven golden lampstands: "I know your works, your labor, your patience, and that you cannot bear those who are evil. And you have tested those who say they are apostles and are not, and have found them liars; and you have persevered and have patience, and have labored for My name's sake and have not become weary. Nevertheless I have this against you, that you have left your first love. Remember therefore from where you have fallen; repent and do the first works, or else I will come to you quickly and remove your lampstand from its place—unless you repent. But this you have, that you hate the deeds of the Nicolaitans, which I also hate. "He who has an ear, let him hear what the Spirit says to the churches. To him who overcomes I will give to eat from the tree of life, which is in the midst of the Paradise of God.'" — Revelation 1:20-27

Let us consider Jesus' words to the seven churches in the first three chapters of Revelation.

If you know the book of Revelation at all, you know that it begins with John the Apostle, who is exiled on the Island of Patmos. This is John the beloved, the disciple that Jesus loved. And Jesus gives him a vision. And much of the vision, of course, has to do with the final return of Jesus to earth, the period of tribulation, the rise of the anti-Christ, all of that. And John sees many things in his vision that I'm not going to touch on at all. But I wanted to look at the very beginning couple of chapters in Revelation; Jesus' own words to the seven churches.

Jesus words are the mind of God revealed. And Jesus words and life reveal the love song of God to the people of the earth. I John 4:10 — *"In this is love, not that we loved God, but that He loved us and sent His Son to be the propitiation for our sins."* That word "propitiation" means "satisfaction." Jesus death satisfied the debt of our sin. And the Bible says, *"And not for ours only, but he was the satisfaction for the sins of the whole world."*

The sin debt of the entire world has been paid in Jesus. That means the sin debt of your entire life has already been paid. As you approach Jesus, he isn't waiting for you to come clean on things you've done wrong before he'll talk to you. He isn't standing with arms crossed, waiting for you to admit all the things you've done wrong.

No, Jesus made you right with the God-head. It's only a matter of agreeing with him. Those who agree with him, (those who believe) shall be saved. God is not beholding your sin waiting for your behavior to change. He is beholding His Son, with whom you are seated at the right hand of the Father. And he is filling your cup to overflowing with the goodness of His life in you as you believe. You are seated right now with Christ in the heavenlies. And your Father is pleased with you; enter into his pleasure. Enter into his influence.

And you really, really must know that and believe it in order to approach the book of Revelation; otherwise, you'll be thrown off. If you don't understand your position in Christ as a redeemed and pleasing Son or Daughter of your Father, if you don't get that, you will misinterpret the first 3 chapters of revelation.

You, as a believer in Jesus, are loved. You are loved and whole and perfected forever in Christ, You are the beloved son of the Father in whom he is well-pleased, right now. Say right now to yourself, "I am well-pleasing to my Father." If you are in Christ, that's what he says. God says to his Son; *"Here is my beloved son in whom I am well-pleased."* If you have faith in Jesus, your Father is well-pleased with you.

See, you have to carry that central truth with you into the book of Revelation. If you don't it'll mess you up; you'll get the message of Revelation wrong. And that is especially true of the first 3 chapters.

So let's look at this. The apostle John is having a vision while he is praying. And he sees Jesus, and Jesus is walking among seven lampstands, which are the seven churches in Asia-Minor at that time. Look at chapter 1 verse 20. This is Jesus talking. *"The mystery of the seven stars which you saw in my right hand, and the seven golden lampstands: the seven stars are the angels* (literally "messengers" — these are the pastors of the churches; these are the preachers; the ones delivering the messages; Jesus has them in his right hand. What a wonderful, secure place to be!); *"and the seven lampstands which you saw are the seven churches."*

These seven churches are examples for us to learn by. These churches did some things really well, and some things they did poorly. But get this right: the church collective, these congregations, *not individuals*, are being judged by Jesus. These are institutions that are being judged by Jesus. The lampstand, the institution, as the carrier of Jesus' light, is being judged. Not you! Not you! You are not being judged here.

So if you're seeing a harsh word in Revelation to the church, it's not being directed to individual believers, it's being directed to the leaders of these churches, as instruction on how to do things better. Now, we all know that the local church itself, as an institution, does stupid things now and again. That imperfect institution is not Jesus. Amen!? Your church is not Jesus.

Where is Jesus? Jesus is in his individual people. Think about this. You are NOT the lampstands in a certain place. That lampstand is just a collection of decisions that we all make together. That lampstand is not you. Where are you in this?

Consider with me. This vision John is having is of Jesus walking about the churches on the earth. Where is Jesus right now? The Bible says that he ascended into heaven. That's Acts chapter one. And yet here in this vision, John is seeing Jesus walk among these churches.

If Jesus is in heaven, then how is Jesus also on the earth? The only place Jesus exists on the earth is in you. His Holy Spirit in you!!

Listen, the Jesus that is walking among the lampstands/churches is the Jesus that is in his people. Let me say it another way. This picture of Jesus walking in and among his church, is a picture of *you* inspecting the lampstands of the church, not a picture of Jesus inspecting you. Jesus, in God's people, is inspecting the lampstand (the lampstand is that which holds up the light). Some lampstands (some churches) do a poor job of holding up the light, and they really, really, should be removed. Who does the removing? You do! Every believer votes with their feet, don't they?

I mean, can we all agree that the church as an institution has done lots of dumb things. And to the church in Ephesus, Jesus says he's going to take the lampstand that is the church institution at Ephesus, and remove it. That's God's people abandoning a church that has lost its first love.

Some churches just deserve to die. They should be dead. Do not call the ambulance. Pin a do not resuscitate order to the front door. You know what I'm saying.

Okay, so these messages to the churches in Ephesus, Smyrna, Pergamos, Thyratira, Sardis, Philadelphia, Laodicea, are the thoughts of Jesus through his own people toward the institutions that are supposed to be lifting up his light (his truth on the lampstands).

So the seven lampstands are the seven churches in Asia Minor. They are represented by lampstands. What do lampstands do? They carry a light. They are meant to be lights in the world (the light of Jesus in this world). Could we agree that some churches don't do a very good job of lifting Jesus' light to the world? Would it be a sad thing for them to be removed? Uh-uh.

So what we're seeing in the book of Revelation here is Jesus speaking through his people to offer encouragement, exhortation, and even rebuke, to the lampstands, the individual churches, the carriers of the light of Jesus to this world.

See, this has always been interpreted backwards. These words to the churches have been delivered by pastors to the people as stern warnings. "You better get these things right! Look what you are doing wrong! You're lukewarm! Shape up!" But it's really just the opposite. It's Jesus' (through his people) saying to the leaders of the churches (the angels, the messengers), "We need you to get this right. Here's where it's good, here's where it's not good. Let's work on this."

The point is this (and you really must embrace this to understand Revelation); this is not Jesus saying to you as an individual, "I will remove your lampstand from my presence if you don't straighten up and fly right." No! It's you, with the eyes of Jesus, yearning for your church to be the bright light on the lampstand that shines out gloriously for the sake of this world!

Now a church, a congregation, is judged on the basis of its works. That's the only way an institution can be judged. So let's look at how the church in Ephesus was doing.

Verse 2 — "*I know your works, your labor, your patience, and that you cannot bear those who are evil.* (*Bearing those who are evil*; the image is of the church carrying them along. You don't allow those who haven't experience Jesus to just go along and not experience him.) *And have tested those who say they are apostles and are not, and have found them liars; and have persevered and have patience, and have labored for My name's sake and have not become weary.*"

Okay, those are the things that the institutional church in Ephesus was doing right, as a congregation. That's what the leaders had led this body of believers into. It sounds a bit exhausting. "I've seen your works, your labor, testing, persevering, labored (again), not become weary."

Look at this. This is as much praise as Jesus can find here, and it's pretty limited. A limited praise report. It's a list of doing. Some of the doing was good, and even needed. But Jesus is not impressed. There is no heaping of praise here. Something central is missing. Remember, this is God's people in Jesus, judging the church.

Here's what missing, verse 4, *"Nevertheless I have this against you, that you have left your first love."* Wow, read that again, *"you have left your first love."*

Just think about this. The first love of a church is not your love for Jesus, it's Jesus love for you. It's 1 John 4:19; *"We love because he first loved us."* Whose love was first? Jesus' love. And in this church in Ephesus, the leadership was trading in the message of Jesus' love for you, and replacing it with your love for Jesus.

The message preached in Ephesus had degenerated into "love God! Love God! Love God!" That's the first and foremost commandment in the Bible. *"Love God with all your heart soul mind and strength."*

But the human soul is not capable of initiating love for God on its own. You can't love God without first experiencing his love for you. *We love,* the bible says, *because he first loved us.* And it isn't just initially that way. It is perpetually that way. We continue loving God because we continue to experience his love. The leaders in Ephesus were preaching, "love God, love God, love God." But you can't conjure up love for God out of human effort. You cannot love God without him first pouring his love into you. *Here is love, not that we loved God, but that He loved us!*

When you receive the first love of "He loves you," then you have the love in you to love God back; and it isn't any effort at all (you don't have to command it; it simply rises up). But if you leave your first love; that is, God's love for you; if that's not first ALL THE TIME, then all you have left for God is, at best, resentful obedience. "I'm serving you, God, because I'm terrified of going to hell. And I'll try to be good for you, because I've got your sword hanging over my head which is your angry wrath at my wrongdoing that will send me to hell if I'm not careful." Serving God out of fear inevitably brings hatred.

You see, I've always heard this passage interpreted exactly that way; which is exactly backwards. Jesus says in verse 5, *"Remember therefore from where you have fallen; repent and do the first works, or else I will come to you quickly and remove your lampstand from its place — unless you repent."* I have heard this preached in a way that bullies God's people! And the antidote that I've heard preached is, "You need to love God more. Come on, where is your love. Show it to me. If you don't return to your first love, your lampstand will be removed." And people respond out of shame or guilt and put money in the offering, or do religious looking things; but in the end, it just brings resentment and hatred toward God as you try to earn his love.

Repent of that! Okay, "repent" means to change the way you think. Jesus says, you're thinking wrongly! "Remember from where you have fallen." Falling means you are going from a high, high place, to a low, low place." They've gone from high place of emphasizing God's amazing love for them; to a much lower place of emphasizing their love and service for God.

Nothing good starts from the place of you trying to love God. Do you know what starts from the place of your love for God? Angry religious fanaticism. Angry austerity that wears the mask of religion. Do this, don't do that. Wear this, don't wear that. St. Paul says in Colossians 2:23, *"These things indeed have an*

158

appearance of wisdom in self-imposed religion, false humility, and neglect of the body, but are of no value. . ."

Every good thing, including your love for God, has its origins in "God loves you and gave himself as a ransom to buy you back." Experience his love. Live in his love. Swim in his love. This is your first love. Return to it. The first love, you see, is not your love. No, God initiates. The first love is *his* love.

Listen to me. God is not looking for some human effort on your part to conjure up pseudo-love for him. No, his love is first. Return to it. Returning to the love that HAD YOU at the first. The love that CAPTURED YOU! It's a returning to the greatest miracle news of the Bible; "Jesus love me, this I know, for the Bible tells me so." Start there. Pretty soon it'll be, "Jesus loves me this I know because I have experienced it so." Your faith in his love cracks open the door to *experiencing it*. And if you begin to give yourself over to this one singular truth, "Jesus loves me. Jesus loves me. He loves me and he's not holding anything against me. He loves me. Not, "he loves me if I do . . .)

No, no. He loves you. Let him. Let him! Let him love you! Receive it. You receive his love by receiving his truth over you. He is holding none of your wrongdoings against you. *"God was in Christ, reconciling the world to himself."* Are you in the world? Then you were being reconciled to the Father. God was in Christ, *"reconciling the world to himself, not counting their sins against them."* How does that make you feel. God is never, never, never counting your sins against you because he counted all of them against Jesus. For God so loved you, so loved *you*, that he gave his only begotten Son, that whoever believes would have God's quality of life. Whoever believes!

He loves you, man! Just believe. As the door to belief cracks open, his love will flood your soul. Do

159

you believe it? Think about it. He says he loves you. Do you believe it? If you believe it, speak this out; "I have a Father. I have a Papa. And he loves me! I have a Redeemer. And he loves me. Say, "Jesus, I receive your love."

Now you've returned to the love you had at the first.

Without that love, a ministry is toast. Without "the love of God" being the only thing (and you and I just believing it) without that being preached from the pulpit as the primary thing, the ministry is worthless. It is "sounding bronze," as Paul said in I Corinthians 13. It's just judgment that puts people under condemnation.

No, "remember!" says the Lord. Vs. 5 *"Remember from where you have fallen. Repent* (change your mind) *and do the first works."* What was the work you did at the first? You believed. Believe that Jesus is *for* you. Believe him. Believe that he has taken your sin issue out of the way. Believe that you, right now, this very second, based on the work of Jesus alone, are completely acceptable to your heavenly Father. What is the work you did at the first? You believed.

The people once asked Jesus directly, John 6:28-29: *"What must we do to do the works God requires?" Jesus answered, "The work of God is this: to believe in the one he has sent."*

Brothers and sisters, do the work that you did at the first: believe! Believe that Jesus has done it all. Return to the love you had at the first. Whose love? *His!* Don't make *your* love for God the foundation of your life. Make his love for you the foundation of your life.

So Jesus is talking to the leader, the pastor of the church at Ephesus, through the people of the church. And in verse 6, he says something that the leader of the church is doing right. Read this, *"But this you have, that you hate the deeds of the Nicolaitans, which I also hate."*

You know, nobody knows exactly who the Nicolaitans actually were. But their identity is in their name. Nico — means "to control". Laitan — means laity. Laity are the non-clergy. Nicolaitans are those who control the laity. It's a clergy that manipulates the people through guilt, or shame, or avarice, or fear. Controlling people for a certain end. Oh, Jesus hates that!

For people who have experienced that kind of thing in the church and then who finally get set free into the love and grace of Jesus, *they hate that too!* In fact, a lot of people just swear off the church because they refuse to be manipulated again. I have had so many people say to me, "I never thought I'd find myself in a church again. I hate that I was manipulated by guilt. I hate that I was manipulated by fear."

I know. Jesus hates that too. Hates it. For freedom, you have been set free. And now that we have been set free, we will never let that happen to us again. No more manipulation. Only rejoicing. Only rejoicing and responding in joy to the love that was first shown us.

You know, there are seven churches that Jesus speaks to in Revelation. They all have the same basic structure. And they all end this way; *"to him who overcomes . . . ."* and then, a promise that Jesus gives us. And I want to tell you something about the promise. The promise attached to each one of these messages for the one that overcomes is not for the distant future. It is for the here and now, with eternal ramifications attached. It is a gift you receive now that ripples out into eternity.

Revelation 2:7; *To him who overcomes* (in this case, it's to him who can get past the stupidity of the church's mistakes) *I will give to eat from the tree of life, which is in the midst of the Paradise of God.* This is a reference to the Garden of Eden. In the middle of the garden was the tree of life; the tree that brings life. Real life. Eternal life, which is God's quality of life.

And what Jesus was saying to his people was that everyone who overcomes the issue he just talked about, which was not living in your first love; to everyone who overcomes that and gets back to that place where it's you resting in the love of Jesus and his finished work for you; everyone who gets back to that, finds real life. Finds the God-quality of life that was introduced in the garden.

Where God cares for us, we relax and enjoy his care because our confidence is in his love alone. Eat that. That fruit tastes so good.

REVELATION

THE CHURCH AT PERGAMOS

The Apostle John is seeing a vision unfold in his mind's eye. And the first part of this vision is a vision that takes place on earth, with Jesus walking among the seven lampstands which represent the seven churches. And that really is the key. Where is this taking place? On earth. How is Jesus depicted here? He is on earth walking "in the midst" of the seven lampstands. That's Jesus in you. You, as God's people, walk among the seven lampstands. On the earth, Jesus goes where you go because he's in you.

So this picture of Jesus giving messages to the seven churches is the picture of Jesus speaking through the church (his people) to the pastors of these churches, who are represented as stars in his hand.

And this foundational premise is crucial. This is not the way it's been portrayed; where the preacher is going to judge you with Jesus' words from the pulpit; and tell you what you're doing wrong. Followed by warnings and threats that, "if you don't straighten up . . Jesus is going to remove you from your place, or spew you out of his mouth for being lukewarm. No, it's you, God's people, as led by Jesus himself, judging the message and actions of the institutional church through exhortation, encouragement, and rebuke.

SO with that in mind, look at Revelation 2:12, *"And to the angel of the church in Pergamos write, 'These things says He who has the sharp two-edged sword:"*

Just to clarify, this is Jesus speaking; and Jesus has the sharp two edged sword. But it's not a physical sword, is it? This is symbol language. John describes

Jesus this way just a few verses earlier. Here is the picture, Revelation 1:16 — *"He had in his right hand seven stars, out of his mouth went a sharp two edged sword."* That's just a weird picture to think about; out of Jesus' mouth came a sword. But it's simply meaning that the sword of Jesus is his words.

Christ's own words to us cut to the division of soul and spirit; in other words, they open us up to our very core, the place where spirit and soul intersect, which is our heart; what we truly believe. Jesus is wanting us to look at what we truly believe about ourselves and about him.

Verse 13 reads;*"I know your works, and where you dwell, where Satan's throne is. And you hold fast to My name, and did not deny My faith even in the days in which Antipas was My faithful martyr, who was killed among you, where Satan dwells."* Okay, we know from archeology that the Temple to Zeus was in Pergamos; the Greek God above all gods. So there was plenty of persecution for Christians there, who said that Jesus, not Zeus, was Lord of lords, God of gods.

Verse 14; *"But I have a few things against you, because you have there those who hold the doctrine of Balaam, who taught Balak to put a stumbling block before the children of Israel, to eat things sacrificed to idols, and to commit sexual immorality."*

Now, remember, this is you the people, judging rightly about the doctrine that's being preached out in church. And this is pointing way back to the time when the people of Israel were coming out of the wilderness and beginning to move into the promised land.

That picture of Israel going into the Promised Land is used in the New Testament as a symbol, a picture, of the church entering into it's promised rest in Jesus. And you can read all about that in Hebrews 3 and 4.

The Bible says there is a promised rest for believer's in Jesus. A place where you quit your striving to be good enough for God, a place where you rest in the finished work of Jesus for you, a place where you can know and believe that you have a Father who is taking care of you, a Spirit who is leading you into wise decisions. There is a place of real rest where you just know that you are loved and acceptable. The place where you are putting all your confidence in what Jesus did. A place where you are not striving to be good enough for God. A real place of rest with God in this world (it's for right now!). It's what Jesus said in Matthew 11:28-30; *"Are you tired? Worn out? Burned out on religion? Come to me. Get away with me and you'll recover your life. I'll show you how to take a real rest. Walk with me and work with me, watch how I do it. Learn the unforced rhythms of grace. I won't lay anything heavy or ill-fitting on you. Keep company with me and you'll learn to live freely and lightly."*

That rest, rest with God, where you quit your striving with him, only comes when you KNOW that Jesus has made you righteous, and worthy and acceptable, apart from your doing. It is *his* work. He did it for you. He lives in you and you can rest in what he has done. You are loved by the Father. You are accepted by him. That feels so good to live in that place, amen?

But for many of us, there was a time in our lives as believers in Jesus, when we did not know that. And we struggled with being good enough for God. We were sin focused, never measuring up; not understanding what Jesus did. In other words, we had Jesus, but we did not have his rest!

The Bible describes that very thing in Hebrews 4:1 — *"Therefore since a promise remains of entering*

His rest, let us fear lest any of you seem to have come short of it." See the promise belongs to every believer, but some believers "seem to come short of it." It is theirs, but they never possess it. <u>A stumbling block</u> is in their way.

And that, (right there!), that stumbling block is exactly what Jesus is talking about in his message to the pastor at Pergamos. *"You have there those who hold the doctrine of Balaam, who taught Balak to put a stumbling block before the children of Israel; to eat things sacrificed to idols, and to commit sexual immorality."*

There was something being preached in Pergamos that was a stumbling block to people entering Christ's promised rest. And preachers everywhere have latched onto the *"food sacrificed to idols and sexual immorality,"* as the stumbling block. That was not the doctrine of Balaam. That was the strategy of Balaam. The stumbling block, the goal of Balaam and Balak in the Old Testament story, was to get God's people to embrace the idol Ba'al. It was to have them believe in a different god! That's the stumbling block. *The strategy* was to use the Ba'al worshipping women to seduce the men, so they would eventually embrace a false god.

So Israel, with a mighty army, is ready to move into the promised land! Hallelujah. God had given to them the land as a gift. Everything was ready. They were trusting him to give it to them, even though there are enemies that need defeated. Balak is one of those enemies. He is a gentile king who does not want Israel to possess the land.

He gets Balaam the prophet to curse Israel. But God does not allow Balaam to curse them. And even though Balaam can't curse Israel directly, he gives Balak a different strategy. Get the Israelites to quit trusting their God Yahweh, and start worshiping the idol Ba'al.

And the worshipping of the false god <u>was the stumbling block</u>. Numbers 25:3; *"So Israel was joined to Ba'al of Peor; and the anger of the Lord was aroused against Israel."* Why? Because they began mixing-in the worship of an idol with the worship of Yahweh.

So now, even though God has given them the Promised Land as a gift, they are unable to enter it because of their idolatry. They stopped seeing the true God Yahweh as their source for every good. They added another god, Ba'al. Do you know what Ba'al looks like? There are ancient statues of Ba'al. He is a prideful looking human; just looking down his nose.

So what is happening in the church in Pergamos? They are allowing people to teach a doctrine that is a stumbling block; a doctrine that keeps the people from entering the promised rest; a doctrine that mixes in the prideful man, Ba'al to the finished work of Jesus. The stumbling block is not sexual immorality. As bad as that is, that is not the doctrine of Balaam. The doctrine of Balaam is, "you should add something to Yahweh in order to find rest." You should add something to Jesus finished work in order to better secure the promised land for yourself.

That's a stumbling block. You can't find God's promised rest to you in Jesus if you have a preacher who is telling you that you need to add the prideful man, your own efforts at this. "Do these five things to get God to answer prayer for you. Make sure your life has no sin to get these blessings." No, that is a stumbling block.

It's just more of the same old, same old. Jesus said, verse 15, *"Thus you also have those who hold the doctrine of the Nicolaitans, which thing I hate."* Nico

— control, laitan -laity. Jesus was saying that, in the end, the doctrine of Balaam is just another attempt at the clergy trying to control the laity by adding some works that laity have to do to get blessings from God or be fully approved. And usually somewhere in that list is "write your biggest check." Because *then* God will bless you. God won't bless you unless you plant the seed first. In other words, the promised land really isn't yours as a gift. Approval of God really isn't yours as a gift. The promised rest of Jesus really isn't yours as a gift. You have to do something to get it. Stumbling block! If you have to "do" to enter God's rest and gain approval, you'll never get there. Believe me, so many of us have tried.

And it was only when the stumbling block was removed, and we heard the unmixed, pure gospel of Jesus Christ (that he has done a finished work in you, that we have been perfected forever, that we are right now the righteousness of God, that sin does not cause us to fall out of fellowship with Papa, but that he has made his permanent home in us, unbroken fellowship, all our sins, past present and future already forgiven in Jesus); when we got our heads around that, we finally understood peace! Lasting peace. Joy. Lasting Joy. We finally entered into the our promised rest! Are you resting?

To churches that preach the doctrine of Balaam, Jesus (through his people) says this to you, verse 16; "*Repent* (change your mind) *or else I will come to you quickly and will fight against you with the sword of my mouth.*"

In other words, oh preacher, God's people are going to come to you with the words of Jesus and confront you with the truth, and things are going to get lopped off of you. You are going to abruptly lose some theological parts and, perhaps, some pride. And friends, that is what is happening right now in this reformation, the tidal wave that is rising right now around the world. The reformation of the church, the people who have had the stumbling block removed, they are rising up, and they are going forth and it is an unstoppable tide of rising water. And these people (perhaps even you as a reader of this book!), can't keep your mouths shut. That sword just keeps launching out of your mouth.

You have experienced life and peace in the promised land! Amen! Life is yours right now. Rest is yours right now. You are beloved and forgiven forever. Every blessing is already yours free of charge and apart from the works of the law; apart from the prideful man-god who thinks he can add to what Jesus did.

When you understand that, you receive rest. What you really receive is a new life. And I want to look at the beautiful words of Jesus as he finishes his words to Pergamos.

Verse 17 — *"He who has an ear, let him hear what the Spirit says to the churches. To him who overcomes I will give some of the hidden manna to eat. And I will give him a white stone, and on the stone a new name written which no one knows except him who receives it."*

Okay, to the person who overcomes (that's the person who overcomes the stumbling block that keeps him from entering the promised rest) "*I will give some of the hidden manna to eat.*"

The manna was the food that God gave to Israel in the wilderness. And Jesus said that that food was a picture of himself. He is the manna, he is the bread that comes down out of heaven and gives life to the world.

But why is it called the *hidden* manna. People have struggled with that; but this is just another Old Testament image.

Do you remember that in the time of the wanderings, God instructed the people to build the Ark of the Covenant; The ark of the covenant was just a wooden box overlaid in gold. And God instructed Moses to put three things inside the box. The stone tablets of the Ten Commandments. The rod of Aaron (which was the rod that bloomed and flowered — it was a symbol of the resurrection — the dead stick coming miraculously to life and producing fruit all in a single night; so it symbolized Jesus' resurrection). And what was the third thing in the Ark of the Covenant? The jar of manna.

Now Solomon was the king of Israel who got to build the permanent temple in Jerusalem. The building of the temple was not what God wanted. It was, in the eyes of Israel, the permanent installation of the Covenant of Law into the nation. God said to them, "are you going to build a temple for me? Do you think that's where I want to live? God does not live in a temple made with human hands." He lives in you! Amen? But Solomon builds the temple, and when the temple was going to be dedicated they brought up the Ark of the Covenant to put in the Holy of Holies. And they brought the Ark of the Covenant (the ark of the *Old Covenant of law*). When they brought it into the temple, to permanently enshrine it in the Temple, they opened it up, and guess what they found. I Kings 8:9; *"Nothing was in the ark except the two tablets of stone which Moses put there at Horeb, when the LORD made a covenant with the children of Israel, when they came out of the land of Egypt."*

In other words, the two symbols of the power and presence of Jesus (the rod of Aaron and the heavenly manna) were not in the Ark! God had removed them from the ark and hidden them away until the time of fulfillment. It was God saying, "if you are going to institutionalize the Law Covenant, then it will just be the law. There will be no mixing of Jesus; the power of this resurrection, the life of his presence. I will not allow you to mix Jesus with the law." And all that remained for them to institutionalize was the stone tablets.

God hid away the life in Jesus until the fulfillment of time. And that hidden manna, which is the life of Christ alone, (only manna, apart from the law), that is the gift that God gives to his people. The hidden manna is the symbol of only Jesus. God separated him out from the stone tablets. Just eat him. Just eat that. Eat only Jesus. That is where your life is.

If you are in a church that is feeding you pieces of stone with manna; spit it out. Go to a different church. Manna and stone don't mix. Just manna. Just what Jesus did. That is life. He is life. And hear this now, he is your own life. Jesus is your own true life.

Jesus said if you overcome, if you get to the place where you have ears to hear, and you see that it's only him that you should be feeding on, then "*I will give him a white stone, and on the stone a new name written which no one knows except him who receives it.*"

And this is the most beautiful and profound message in this entire word to the church at Pergamos.

You see, Jesus does give you a stone, but it's not for eating. You know there are three words for stone in the Greek language, *lithos, petros,* and p*sephos*. *Lithos* is used most often (82 times in the New Testament) and it means stone. *Petros* is used 161 times and its most often just transliterated as Peter. But it means rock.

The third word is p*sephos,* and it is used exactly twice in the New Testament. It's used here and it's used in Acts 26:10. Let's read that. Acts 26:10 — this is St. Paul giving his testimony; how before he was saved he persecuted believers. He says, *"This I also did in Jerusalem, and many of the saints I shut up in prison, having received authority from the chief priests; and when they were put to death, I cast my vote against them."* And the word translated there as *vote* is *psephos*. The imagery is that you would judge a person guilty or not guilty by putting your stone in with other people's stones who were deciding a case. If you put in a black *psephos,* a black stone, you were casting a vote of guilty. If you put in a white stone, you were declaring innocence. Your verdict was tied to the color of the stone.

In acts 26, Paul was casting a guilty verdict by putting in the black stone. His vote was against them. Well Jesus has a stone. He has a *psephos*; and it has your name on it. And it is the permanent verdict of your life that he gives to you as gift. And it is white. Because the judgment has been rendered against you. And the judgment is, "innocent!"

And it's more beautiful than that. Jesus says that it is a *white* stone, and it is. But calling the stone white is a gross understatement; it's a bit like saying Bill Gates has a few dollars in the bank. This brings me to tears when I think about it.

The Greek word for white is *aspros*. It's a common word for the color. Jesus said that your stone is *leukos*. *Leukos* is only used a few times in scripture. It's used to describe Jesus at his transfiguration; when it says that his face and his clothes became brilliant, dazzling white, as no fuller on earth could make them. *That* kind of white (dazzling white), *that's leukos*. So it's used there to describe the white of the transfiguration. It's used to describe the white of the resurrection, and it's used one other place, besides Revelation, that I want to show you.

The image of white is a depiction of your righteousness. White is the color of purity. Like Ivory soap white; you know, 99 44/100's percent pure. But it's more than that. It's miracle white. It's like saying something is 200% pure, 200% righteous. And the only other place it's used in scripture is when Jesus was looking at the crowd of people who were coming to him for his teaching. And you remember, from John 4:35, he turns to his disciples as the crowd is nearing and he says, "*Look, I say to you, lift up your eyes and look at the fields, for they are already (leukos) white for harvest!* "They are already" ("I declare them to be") innocent, dazzling white, righteous, pure, innocent for the harvest!

Jesus made the declaration of innocence over the crowd. They were ready to be harvested. Ready to hear and believe. Ready to apply their faith to receive salvation.

When you look out over a crowd of people, you must see them with the eyes of Jesus. They are not sinners in the hands of an angry God, who is waiting for them to repent and confess their sin. But Jesus has spoken forth his verdict over them; "innocent! Innocent!" Take this verdict for yourself. Take the stone he gives to you as a gift. Believe it. Agree with me about your identity.

You identity is not just that you are white with innocence. But you are the white of Jesus in his transfiguration. You are transfiguration white. You are resurrection white. You are white like no human effort, no amount of human bleaching, could ever produce. You are God's glory kind of white. God's righteousness white. And that is the gift that Jesus hands you; his verdict he hands to you.

And I have one other thing I want to point out about this scripture. It's so very important. The brilliant white stone, the declaration and verdict of your innocence that is handed to you as a gift, contains etched into it your true name. The last part of verse 17 *"and on the stone a new name written which no one knows except him who receives it."*

Your name is your identity. The name is the thing. I want you to understand this; it's so important; your name, your identity, who you really are as a person, cannot be known apart from the righteousness of Jesus. We have all etched lies into our hearts. And we truly believe them. "I am short tempered, I am unlovable, I am unlovely, I am an angry person, I am not patient, I am unworthy." Defining ourselves by our "APART FROM JESUS" life. "I am an adulterer, I am a thief, I am greedy. I am a sexual deviant." These are self-images apart from the life of Jesus. These are self-identities born out of our wrestling with the flesh, and acquiescing to the truths that we see *in our flesh*.

I must make this clear this. I bid you hear me in love. One of the greatest misperceptions about Christianity, if I may be precise here to make this point, is that we say that we receive Jesus *into our life* in order to be born again. We have all said that to help folks along in becoming born again and receiving the good news of Jesus. But the idea behind it is that we are *adding* Jesus to *our lives*. Mix a little Jesus into your life; boom, born again.

That's really not it. You don't receive Jesus into YOUR life. You receive Jesus AS your life. There is no life but in him. Many believers spend their entire lives trying to fix up the old man, which is impossible because Jesus says he's dead. God is not into fixing up the person you decided you were under your time of condemnation and guilt. He is not into fixing up the carnal man. That man died on the cross in Christ. The new life that you possess, the life that is born from above, the life that is the real you, your true identity is *Christ alive in you*!

He gives you your identity. It's written on your verdict stone. Your new name. And that name, that real you, your true identity, is not foreign to you at all, but Jesus says you will recognize it as being the real you. It may not be an identity that anyone else would recognize in you. But when you get your name from him, he says, no one will *"know"* it but the one receiving it.. That person will *"know"* it. You will know it; you will recognize it as the real you.

Who is the real you. Paul said, *"it is no longer I who live, but Christ who lives in me." That* is the real you; the you that you were made to be.

Listen, I was the guy in High School who would never raise my hand in class. I was a total wall-flower. I was turned inward, shy and backward. One time in high school Geometry Class, near the end of the year, my Geometry teacher stood up in class and said, "There's one person in this class who has never said a single word all year long. Can anyone tell me who that is?" And all fingers in the class pointed to me. It was me. I thought I would die. I was the shy one.

I could just resign myself to be that; to make that the definition, the identity of Greg Riether. But you know what? I like the identity that comes with Jesus much better. It is the real me. The real Greg Riether is the guy that stands up every Sunday and boldly declares the love of a savior and the innocence of humanity. Jesus introduced me to myself. It came with the pronouncement of my fiery bright innocence.

Don't let anyone else define you. Jesus knows who you really are. Say to him, Jesus, I do not want the life that I have constructed for myself, I want you alone, living in me, to give me my identity. It is no longer I who live but you who lives in me. With the innocent verdict of the white stone comes another gift from Jesus; He shows you who you really are. And it fits like a glove. Let Jesus introduce you to your true self. What a gift. It is never too late to start learning who you are.

It starts with innocence. You are declared innocent. You are righteous. You are worthy. You are able. You are wise. You are fit for the kingdom. Papa is proud of you for your gallant faith that goes against what others are saying. You are his beloved. You belong to him forever. You are confident, and capable, and beautiful, and lovely, and lovable, and loving, and patient, kind, good, faithful, self-controlled, chaste, joyful, peaceful, gentle. Believe *him*. Let him introduce you to yourself.

REVELATION
THE CHURCH AT THYATIRA

And to the angel of the church in Thyatira write: 'These things says the Son of God, who has eyes like a flame of fire, and His feet like fine brass: "I know your works, love, service, faith and your patience; and as for your works, the last are more than the first. Nevertheless I have a few things against you, because you allow that woman Jezebel, who calls herself a prophetess, to teach and seduce My servants to commit sexual immorality and eat things sacrificed to idols. And I gave her time to repent of her sexual immorality, and she did not repent. Indeed I will cast her into a sickbed, and those who commit adultery with her into great tribulation, unless they repent of their deeds. I will kill her children with death, and all the churches shall know that I am He who searches the minds and hearts. And I will give to each one of you according to your works. "Now to you I say, and to the rest in Thyatira, as many as do not have this doctrine, who have not known the depths of Satan, as they say, I will put on you no other burden. [25] But hold fast what you have till I come. And he who overcomes, and keeps My works until the end, to him I will give power over the nations—'He shall rule them with a rod of iron; They shall be dashed to pieces like the potter's vessels'—as I also have received from My Father; and I will give him the morning star. "He who has an ear, let him hear what the Spirit says to the churches. "— Revelation 2:18-29

Now remember, Jesus is walking in the midst of these seven churches on the earth. That's the vision that John is seeing. Jesus in the midst of the institutional churches is a picture of God's people. Jesus is only present on earth in you. That's why he is walking among all of the seven churches simultaneously. So the picture here is that Jesus, through his people, is judging each of these churches, each of these institutions. He is judging their doctrine, encouraging, exhorting and rebuking. And if a lampstand (a church) needs to be removed, Jesus will remove it; and he does that through you! God's people are the ones deciding which churches remain; you vote with your feet and your pocketbook. And some churches, in Jesus view, just deserve to die.

So here we are in a place called Thyatira. And Jesus is speaking through God's people to the pastor of Thyatira. He is speaking about this ministry. And the ministry is doing some things right; operating in love, and service and faith and patience. But then, there are things that are not so good at this church.

They tolerate *"that woman Jezebel, who calls herself a prophetess to teach and seduce my servants to commit sexual immorality and eat things sacrificed to idols."*

Now, right away, we know that Jesus is speaking in symbol language. I mean, the story of Jezebel comes out of the Old Testament. She was the Ba'al worshiping wife of King Ahab, the king of Israel. And because he married her, Ahab and all of Israel began worshipping a false God.

And Jesus is referencing this story as a symbol of what's going on in the church. There is a person in this church who has been given a prominent place. She is a prophetess. A prophetess is someone who claims to speak for God. So this person is claiming to speak for

God. But she is actually *not* speaking for God, she is speaking for a false image (understanding) of God. That's what Jezebel does. She speaks for a god who is not God and she causes God's people to believe wrongly.

Now, I have to say, I have heard and read absolutely bizarre things about this whole Jezebel thing. I've heard people say, "This person has a Jezebel spirit." And you can get online and type in "Jezebel spirit" and you will enter a world of theology that talks about demonic sexual control and all kinds of things that legalists want you to keep your eyes on. People in touch with a *spirit of Jezebel* theology want you to watch for particular sin. Legalists always want you to be sin focused. God wants us to be Jesus focused. Jesus said *"do this in remembrance of me."* "Think about what I've done, not what you've done."

And depending on how legalistic you are, you'll get certain things that you should "watch out" for with this Jezebel spirit. Watch out! "Women, don't use make-up, because Jezebel in the Old Testament used make up on the day she died. And if you use make-up, you are opening yourself to a Jezebel spirit." And just extrapolate that out; we're really talking about any kind of thing that enhances sexiness or beauty. Because, obviously, God prefers ugly. Ugliness is next to godliness! Watch out for mascara. Watch out how you fix your hair, the clothes you wear, the shoes you wear (how high are the heals — because flats are godly, two inch heels are pushing the envelope of your Christian freedom, but five inch heels are entering into sin). Watch out for the color of your lipstick, the length of your finger nails, the length of your dress. Doing all the beautiful womanly stuff in order to influence men and bring control.

I just want to be clear here. That is NOT what Jesus is talking about. This is symbol language. And when Jesus says that Jezebel the prophetess is (verse 20) *"seducing my servants to commit sexual immorality,"* he is not saying that a female is painting herself up in order to get men to commit adultery.

Think about this; every other reference to sexual immorality in the book of Revelation is clearly symbolic. And no bible scholar, legalistic or not, would disagree with me on that. But when it comes to Jesus' words to the churches, preachers everywhere take what Jesus clearly meant as a symbol and make it literally. Preachers love heaping condemnation on people over all things sexual.

But Jesus uses the symbol language of sexual immorality to communicate another idea. Think about what Jesus said to the Pharisees; "you wicked and adulterous generation." That does not mean that they were committing sexual immorality. They were Pharisees! They would *never* commit adultery. But Jesus says they are all adulterous. What does this mean? Jesus is saying that their adultery is in not being intimate with the God who is. Rather, they are intimate with stone tablets. They are trading in the God who stood before them (Jesus) for a false God.

And that is exactly what Jesus is saying here. There was a teaching in Thyatira given by a false prophet who claimed to be speaking for Jesus. But this person was not teaching the people to be intimate with Jesus. This person was teaching the people to be intimate with a false god. This person would *"teach and seduce my servants to commit sexual immorality."* Now listen, the end result of that is (verse 20) *"that they would eat things sacrificed to idols."*

That phrase defines the false god. They are eating what they sacrifice to their idol. Let me say it another way; they are feeding on, they are seeking to find their nourishment in, the sacrifices they make to their idol; their false understanding of God. To eat what you sacrifice is to seek to be nourished and built up on your *doing*.

A sacrifice to a god is the thing that a person *does* or *offers* to God in exchange for God's favor. So you offer a sacrifice in order to get God to move on your behalf. The bigger the need, the bigger the sacrifice. And the moment a person does that, what are they putting their faith in? They're putting their faith in their sacrifice. They are putting their hope in their offering. I'll tell you something, whatever you put your hope in, that is your God. And if your hope is in the thing that you do to get God to answer your prayer (or you are counting on the sacrifice of your right behavior as the way to get God to like you), you are offering sacrifice to the false God of yourself. You are seeking to draw nourishment from your own sacrifice. You are feeding on the nourishment of your sacrifice. You are eating your own sacrifice. Brother, there is no nourishment there. You're putting your faith in what you have done.

That's what Jezebel the prophetess was teaching. Eat your sacrifice. Put your faith in your *doing* in order to get God to move on your behalf. "Here is the list of things to do to get what you want from God. Do this." Do you understand what this is saying about nourishing on the things you sacrifice? That is Jezebel's teaching. And Jezebel the prophetess is tolerated in nearly every church to some degree. In fact, Jezebel the prophetess is celebrated in many churches all over the world today.

If anyone stands up before God's people and tells them the list of things they must do to get God to like them, or to keep God liking them; or to get God to answer a prayer request, or "here is how you increase your blessing, do this;" they are causing God's people to enter into adultery. They are causing people to be intimate with an idol. Because the people who are listening to them preach will put their hope in something they've done. They will eat the thing they sacrifice in an attempt to draw spiritual nourishment. But the FACT of the power of Christ's work is that we have already been given *every spiritual blessing in the heavenlies* (Ephesians 1:3). That word "every" means "every" or it's wrong. Has God not already opened his hand to you? Is heaven not already an open heaven? That is the new and living way in Jesus. Everything else is an adulteration.

I was talking to a brother last week. He works on the prayer lines for a major ministry in this country. And one of the most heartbreaking calls he gets is one that is repeated on a daily basis by the desperate people on the other end of the line. "I don't understand; I gave sacrificially to your ministry. I gave my money. But I'm still behind on my mortgage," or "my landlord is getting ready to be kick me out of my apartment." or "my car got repossessed. And I did what you said. Where's my miracle?"

No! No! Don't put your hope in some sacrifice you make. Don't nourish yourself on that. Put your hope, all of it, in the sacrifice Jesus made. Nourish yourself on that! Eat Jesus. Jesus has done it all. He was the sacrifice that made things right between you and your Papa God. He made things right eternally. You are eternally redeemed (Hebrews says). Eternally forgiven. Eternal blessed with every blessing in the heavenlies. You are perfected forever. That's the sacrifice of Jesus. Eat that. Digest what Jesus has done. There is a never ending supply of Jesus to meet every need that manifests.

Do not put your hope in your offering. Do not put your hope in your piety. Put your hope in Jesus' finished work. Finished work! Finished. "It is finished," he said. That means you can't add a sacrifice of your own. If you are thinking you need to add a sacrifice, you have let Jezebel speak to you.

Look. What do you need right now? Here's my list of five steps for you to do to get your answer from God. 1) Behold Jesus. 2) Behold Jesus. 3) Behold Jesus. 4) Behold Jesus. 5) Behold Jesus. "Jesus you are in me. You are my righteousness. As you are, so am I in this world, right now. You are healed. You are peaceful. You are prospering. You are worthy. You are perfected forever. I feed on your sacrifice. I am healed. I am peaceful. I am prospering. I am worthy. I am perfected forever." Put your hope there! All of it.

Do not tolerate the Jezebel. Jesus says (verse 22-23; this is what he thinks) *"I will cast her into a sickbed, and those who commit adultery with her into great tribulation, unless they repent of their deeds. I will kill her children with death."* Now remember, as Jesus is talking about children, that this is the same Jesus who says, *"Let the little children come to me . . ."* Jesus is not talking about human children here. Jesus is saying this; "the ministry of Jezebel will be sickly and bent and without power. Those who enter adultery with her, those who believe her foolishness, will enter into *"great tribulation."* (Isn't that the truth! There is no peace in the message that mixes the Old Covenant of Law with the New Covenant of Grace). And what this means when Jesus says, *"I will kill all her children with death,"* is that all of the children of Jezebel, all of the *ministries* that are birthed from her theology will die."

The children of Jezebel are the ministries that are birthed from a mixture message of "a little grace, a little works. You come to Jesus by grace, but you have to maintain the relationship by works." It comes in a variety of flavors. Don't eat it. Spit it out. Let those ministries be accursed. Jesus wants those ministries to die. The world is a better place if they die. Those ministries are teaching people to commit adultery. Those ministries are teaching people to be intimate with both Jesus and an idol of their own works and sacrifices.

But there is no power in those ministries. Those ministries have no power to free people into the freedom of Jesus. On the contrary, they bring great tribulation to many of God's people. They are sickly, deathbed ministries.

Do you see how this message here for Thyatira is all about intimacy with Jesus? Oh, and now I begin to get to the good part. This so blesses me!

Verse 26, *"And he who overcomes, and keeps My works until the end, to him I will give the power over the nations."* Don't fly by this. Jesus says *"to he who overcomes."* Who overcomes what? The adultery of mixing anything with Jesus. He says, to *"he who overcomes, and keeps My works until the end."*

The word there for *"keep"* means "to guard from loss; to hang onto." This is the person who hangs onto (who guards from loss) Jesus' works. Whose works? Jesus works. Not your works. This is not saying "to the one who does things the way Jesus does them." No, it's not your works. It's Jesus' works. Guarding his work. Guarding the power of his finished work. Do you hear what this is saying?

To the ones who keep close to themselves Jesus' own works (our hope in his works; feeding on his works, knowing nothing but his works, eating the sacrifice he made, not the sacrifice that we make) to THAT ONE, *"I will give the power over the nations."*

The power over the nations. What does that mean? Thankfully, Jesus tells us exactly what that means in the next verse. Verse 27, *"He shall rule them with a rod of iron; They shall be dashed to pieces like the potter's vessels."*

There are many instances in scripture that refer to the rod of iron. The rod of iron is a reference to Jesus' rule. So picture a rod of iron in your mind's eye. What does that thing weigh? Maybe it has an iron ball on the end. It sounds vicious, doesn't it?

But the rod of iron is not used on people. The rod of iron is not used to smash people under the wrath of God. That is not the imagery Jesus gives us. It is used to have a greater rule than the nations, and it is used to smash the nations as pottery is smashed by an iron rod.

Make sure you have the right image here. The nations of the world are symbolized by ceramic pottery. The ceramic pottery is merely a container that gives definition to whatever is inside of it. In the case of a nation, that which is inside the pottery is people. The people are defined in shape and boundary by the pottery. That is their identity, given to them by the pottery that surrounds them. What does Jesus destroy with his rod of iron? The identities (the boundaries and definitions) of the nations.

The power and work of Jesus (his rule!) shatters every man-made boundary and definition. God's people are not bound by nationality. We are one in Christ. That's what that means. If I have five pottery containers filled with water all side by side, those containers define the water and separate water from water. But when I wield the rod of iron, the power of Jesus' gospel, it smashes the man-made definitions to bits. It smashes the man-made identities to bits. And the water experiences its unity in the larger container of Christ, who holds the nations.

This is saying that every man-made definition and identity, every cultural definition, every denominational definition is smashed to dust by the gospel. The gospel puts unlikely people together because the pottery of our manmade identities has been smashed.

And lastly, Jesus says this; *"and I will give to him the morning star."* Actually, the word for morning is literally the word "day time." Jesus is referred to as the day star. Astronomically, the day star is the star that is seen in the day. It's a poetic reference to the sun. And there's only one other New Testament reference to this outside of Revelation, and it's in 2 Peter 1:19. Here, Peter is making reference to the transfiguration of Jesus that happened during Jesus' earthly ministry. Peter saw the transfiguration of Jesus with his own eyes and it confirmed to him Jesus' identity. Now look at verse 19 — *"And so we have the prophetic word confirmed,"* (The prophecy of Jesus as messiah, the son of God is confirmed). *"And so we have the prophetic word confirmed, which you do well to heed as a light that shines in a dark place."* That is the picture of Jesus' own nature, his own glory, shining onto our darkened heart (a heart that hasn't come to know him yet); *"until the day dawns"* (that's a person who has come to faith in Jesus; the good news was spoken to them and the light of Jesus' true nature began to shine in their heart, i.e. the day dawned).

But now what happens? *"And the morning star (or day star — the sun) rises in your hearts."*

This is so beautiful, because this is a real description of what happens in a life when a person comes to faith in Jesus and begins feeding only on his sacrifice. Jesus is likened to the sun that rises higher and higher in the life of a believer. Jesus himself becomes more and more prominent.

And I want to say it this way, because this is the very thing that I have experienced and am so passionate about.

When I finally had the good news of Jesus' finished work sown in my heart and believed it, it was a light that broke forth inside of me. I had been a believer in Jesus all my life, but I did not understand his finished work. The prophetess Jezebel had spoken into my life at an early age. The result was that I was adding my efforts as a way to please and appease God. I really, really thought my performance in holy living was a governing barometer of God's favor and love and pleasure over me. And I could never please God. I looked at my life and found fault at everything; at the kind of husband I was, the kind of father I was, the kind of pastor I was. I didn't pray enough. I didn't give enough. I didn't read the bible enough. And my thoughts always condemned me.

But when God showed me from the Bible that he never loves me or forgives me on the basis of my performance in holiness; when he showed me that all of my sins (past, present and future) had already been forgiven in Jesus (2 Cor. 5:19), and that I was always free and clear to enter into the holy of holies by this new and living way; when he showed me that nothing can now separate me from his love; when he showed me that "there is now NO condemnation" for me; when he showed me that he is never angry with me or rebuking me; when he showed me that I was his beloved son in whom he is well-pleased all the time; when he showed me that his desire is for me to be a showcase of his favor and love for the world to see forever and ever (that's Eph. 2:7!) I entered a new life. All of that is the good news of Jesus; redeemed forever, perfected forever, forgiven forever. I am a son and he wants me to cry out "Abba, papa" to him. When I finally understood that, truly, the light dawned on my life.

And for the first time in my life, I allowed myself to experience the love of God. And a spirit of slavery that leads to fear was replaced by the spirit of adoption and love. That was my birthday, man. I was born that day. Reborn.

And those ideas really, really began setting me free into understanding the bible and understanding who I am. Jesus used his rod of iron and shattered the container of "sinner" I had put myself in. And I got a new identity; "Righteous, Beloved Son of the Living God." Beautiful.

And I thought, "it can't get any better." I was happy for the first time in my adult life. I was truly happy.

But then, something better happened. Jesus gave to me the morning star; which is to say, he gave to me himself. And I must try to put this into words. The good news of Jesus and what he has done is not the prize. But the mystery of the ages, St. Paul said, is what has now been revealed; "Christ in us the hope of glory."

Jesus is in you. He is in you! Now that is a revelation. If you had asked me if Jesus was in me 10 years ago, I would have said, "of course." But the reality of his presence, the experience of his presence; I did not know it. But now, you see, the day star is rising in my heart. This is exactly what Peter was talking about.

And now I lay on my bed and I think, "Jesus, you're in me. And I declare with your word that it is no longer I who live but only your life in me; that's all I want." And that's the prize! And friend, if you miss that, you miss the prize.

If you miss this, you get people saying ridiculous things. People who say, "well, this grace message means I can just do any sin I want and God will forgive me." No! Stop. God forbid! Jesus has taken up residence in your body and joined himself to you. He is only righteous. He is only holy. I want nothing to do with sinful behavior.

And he is so good, and so loving, and so powerful, and so full of healing. Truly, sometimes I think, "how can my body get sick? How could this mortal frame abide sickness at all with him inside of me? How could I not be led of him when I acknowledge his presence. He's all there is in me.

I am a holy thing. You are a holy thing. The glory of Jesus is all over you. Innocent, righteous, perfect. I tell you, you are perfect, worthy, and whole. Those are mere words describing something you can only experience. Every bit of understanding of Jesus' finished work leads to one nearly indescribable revelation; the Daystar has been given to you. And the more you lay on your bed and come to grips with Jesus reality in you (and who you are now in him!), the higher the daystar rises in your heart.

And that is Christianity. And everything else is a dunghill by comparison. That intimacy is unbroken and covenanted. The realization of that is the Daystar rising higher and higher in your life. Let Jezebel be cursed. Feed on Jesus presence, and his work.

REVELATION
THE CHURCH AT SARDIS

"And to the angel of the church in Sardis write, 'These things says He who has the seven Spirits of God and the seven stars: "I know your works, that you have a name that you are alive, but you are dead. Be watchful, and strengthen the things which remain, that are ready to die, for I have not found your works perfect before God. Remember therefore how you have received and heard; hold fast and repent. Therefore if you will not watch, I will come upon you as a thief, and you will not know what hour I will come upon you. You have a few names even in Sardis who have not defiled their garments; and they shall walk with Me in white, for they are worthy. He who overcomes shall be clothed in white garments, and I will not blot out his name from the Book of Life; but I will confess his name before My Father and before His angels. 'He who has an ear, let him hear what the Spirit says to the churches.'" —Revelation 3:1-6

Okay, let's remember that this is a picture of Jesus on the earth; Jesus in the midst of the seven churches. How is Jesus present on the earth? He is present in his people. That's how Jesus is present in the midst of all seven churches at the same time. So this is really a picture of God's people speaking to the pastors of each of these churches, and judging these institutional churches; rebuking, exhorting, and encouraging. And sometimes even threatening to remove these ministries altogether because of the rotten things that are being proclaimed.

And each of these words of Jesus to the pastors follows a certain pattern. And the beginning of that pattern is that Jesus tells each church what they are doing right, followed by what the churches need to correct. And the church at Sardis has the dubious honor of being only one of two churches in which Jesus could find nothing right! There was nothing worthy of praise going on in this church! In fact, Jesus just starts off with these words, verse 1; *"I know your works, that you have a name that you are alive, but you are dead."*

Okay, this is very telling. He says, "I know your works." This church is producing works. And the works that they are producing must have been some wonderful works because they are causing the people who look on to say, "now THAT church is really alive. THAT church is really doing some wonderful things."

So when people heard the name; "First Christian Church, downtown Sardis," that name was synonymous with "Living Church." "You want to know how to do church? Just do church the way Sardis does church. Because they are alive!"

Now what do believers mean when they say that a church is really alive? It could mean a lot of different things. But typically, what's happening is that people are seeing the fruit of a church, they are seeing some evidences of growth, or movement, or good works, and they are saying, "that fruit is God's fruit. God is blessing them. They are doing all these things right." Their attendance numbers are big. Their offering numbers are big. They've built this nice building. They have nice facilities. They have tons of programming. They have tons of social ministries; they feed the poor, they clothe the naked, etc, etc… Those are good things. Amen?

Nothing wrong with any of those things at all. Those things are fruit. They are works. But people are looking at the fruit; people are looking at the works; and by virtue of the fruit that they see, they have put the name (the identity, the label) of "Alive" on this church.

Jesus sees the same fruit, sees exactly the same works, the same good things that others are seeing, and he puts the name "Dead" on the church, as its identity; it's *true* identity.

They're looking at the same fruit; the same good works, and they are coming up with two polar opposite conclusions. So what's going on here? How is it possible to see the same exact fruit; and PEOPLE look at the fruit and say "living church" but JESUS looks at the fruit and says "dead church." How is that possible?! What is Jesus seeing in the works that most people are not seeing in the works?

Verse 2 — *"Be watchful, and strengthen the things which remain, that are ready to die, for I have not found your works perfect before God"*. The good works produced in the church at Sardis were not "perfect works" before God. There's the fault.

Okay . . . Now at this point, the legalist preacher would determine that the impurity must be due to people slacking off in some way. And so the legalist preacher will step in and say, "hey, you people! You need to purify your hearts. You need to get in a better place with God so that your works will be more pure. You need to get right, get your priorities right, and then give it your ALLLLLL. Give 110% of your effort to God, and then your works will be more acceptable; your works will become perfected before God." And that is exactly how I've heard this preached.

But guess what; that's not the remedy that Jesus prescribes. Jesus prescription for producing perfect works was not "work harder." It's the very next verse, verse 3, *"Remember therefore how you have received and heard; hold fast and repent."*

"Remember," says the Lord! Reach back in your memories and remember the way this works with me. Remember how you have received and heard. Go all the way back. How did you receive from God? How did you receive Jesus? *"By grace through faith."* Jesus was given to you as a gift that you received by faith. How did you become righteous? You received righteousness as a gift, apart from the works of the law; apart from your efforts at doing. It was all God. What about joy? Can you hear Jesus say, "Do you remember when my joy rose up in your heart after you received the good news, and you realized you were forgiven forever? Did you work at it? Did it come because you obeyed a work of the law; or because you just received? That's fruit! That's my fruit being born in you! That's *perfect* fruit that I bore in you."

See, Jesus is saying to them, "if it's me doing the work (bearing the fruit) then it's perfect fruit. If it's you doing good things for any other reason except that it's born in you from above to do it, then it's imperfect fruit. It's you doing it. It's you trying to add something to my finished work.

"As you therefore have received Christ Jesus the Lord, so walk in Him, [7] rooted and built up in Him and established in the faith, as you have been taught, abounding in it with thanksgiving." Colossians 2:6-7.

How did you receive? By faith. How do we walk out the rest of our lives? By faith.

This is really beautiful. How does a believer know what to do in life? How do we receive and participate in works that are perfected works before the Father. Here it is; *"So walk in him, rooted and built up in Him and established in the faith."* That's intimacy talk. We become intimate with our groom. You put your roots deep into Jesus. You let Jesus build you up and pour into you. And in *that* place, you hear the voice of God.

You know the Holy Spirit speaks to you. Christ's own spirit. Don't be thinking like a lot of believer's think, "Oh I wish the Holy Spirit would speak to me and guide me like he does this person over here." He does! Yes. I'll tell you how to listen to the spirit that is speaking to you right now. You meditate on your intimacy with Jesus. Of course, you can meditate on all kinds of other things, and get lots of bad ideas; greed, envy, lust, lack, what a loser you are, how messed up you are. If you meditate on those things you will get whacked out ideas. But when you are in the place of rootedness in Jesus, you hear from God. It's this simple.

He is in you. You find your identity in him, ("*rooted and grounded in him*") your rootedness in him ("Jesus, you love me, I am righteous, holy, worthy, accepted, loved, perfected . . in you, Jesus!"). That's being rooted and built up in Him; in the reality of his presence and the reality of his very being that inhabits you. He is in you. And then, *in that place*, you just consider things. Ask him about things or just be open to new ideas.

That is probably happening right now without you even being aware of it. It is absolutely effortless. I'll tell you the truth; I never think better thoughts than when I am listening to a message that is speaking out the Gospel of Jesus, my Lord, because it puts me right in Jesus' presence.

I get my best ideas while I'm listening to a message that is speaking out the good news of Jesus over me. Oftentimes, I'll just be listening to the good news and the reality of Christ's presence in me becomes so poignant. And in that place, Jesus will show me something, something from scripture that I've been meditating on, or I'll get an idea for something. That's God! That's God! You say, "no it isn't, that's just you thinking creatively." No, that' how God thinks! He thinks in me! We are one. When I am in that place, I feel what he feels, I think what he thinks. Is it me or is it God? Yes! Yes! And in that place I will write things down in my notepad because I don't want to forget them. Some of the things I write down are things that I can do! And then, as St. Paul says, "abounding in thanksgiving," I set out to do what God has purposed in my heart. And THAT THING is not a toil. It's a joy! And the joy within me is a confirmation that this, indeed, is the Lord who has spoken to me. I am so thankful to God when I hear clearly from him. *"So walk in Him, rooted and built up in Him and established in the faith, as you have been taught, abounding in it with thanksgiving.*

When you live that way, you produce perfect fruit, because the fruit is born out of intimacy with Jesus, your groom.

If you are trying to produce fruit in any other way, (from any other motive) you are producing imperfect fruit. If you are thinking that you must do this thing, this work, because this is going to help your relationship with God; that's imperfect fruit. Think about it, how many times have you done things out of guilt before God. The Bible says that Jesus' fruit abounds with thanksgiving. You can't be abounding in thanksgiving and abounding in guilt at the same time. It doesn't work.

Guilt produced fruit is imperfect fruit. In fact, Paul says it much more harshly than that. He uses the example of Abraham and the fruit he produced through Sarah and Hagar. God told Abraham that he would have a promised son through Sarah. But it didn't happen right away, so Sarah and Abraham agreed that he should be intimate with Sarah's handmaiden, Hagar, and produce a son through her. And that's what he did. But the fruit of that union was not God's fruit. It was the fruit of human effort. Now stop and think. That union between Abraham and Hagar produced real fruit. It was a real human son, Ishmael, who was produced. But it was not the work of God that produced it, (nor was it God's solution). Rather, it was the efforts of man and it was man's solution to a need.

And Paul uses that as a powerful illustration of mixing in your manmade efforts to what God wants to accomplish. Paul says, *"cast out the bondwoman, cast out Hagar and her children!"* Cast out your manmade efforts! It's just adultery. Don't go down that path. The fruit it produces is not God's fruit, it's your fruit.

And the church, as an institution, is so fruit obsessed that it often doesn't care where the fruit comes from, as long as you're producing fruit. No. No, that's all wrong. God does want to produce fruit through you, but he wants it to be fruit that comes from intimacy with him.

As an example, it's comparable to my wife and I wanting to have children. Let's say we wanted more children but were unable to because something was wrong with me. But one day she comes home and says to me, "Greg, rejoice, I'm pregnant!" I would say, "Really, how did that happen?" "Oh, I was intimate with an old high school flame of mine. But isn't this great; we're having a baby." I would say, "No, that's not great! *We're* not having a baby. *You're* having a baby. The baby is not *our* baby." The point is not just that there's fruit. The point is that there would be OUR FRUIT.

But this is the problem with many churches. They produce fruit, but its fruit that is born in intimacy with something other than Jesus. And so, "praise the Lord, we had ten people come forward and rededicate their lives to Jesus because I preached Jonathan Edwards revival sermon that they are sinners in the hands of an angry God, dangling above the flames of hell by a mere thread. And I scared them into the kingdom. Praise God. Hallelujah, God is good." Wait a minute! That's fear-based evangelism. You've just produced people who are relating to God on the basis of fear, not on the basis of love! That's not God's fruit. You've just produced fruit out of your own flesh. And fruit that is produced in the flesh must be maintained by the flesh. The only way to keep those believers motivated is to increase the fear factor. Hey, that church should be a new TV show. Fear Factor Church!

Sorry to say this, but Jonathan Edwards of the so-called *great awakening* in this country (that revival that so many want to duplicate), he is no hero of mine. He did not free people into the gospel of Christ. He enslaved them again to the spirit of fear. If there was any good that came out of it, it's only that some people were able to grow past that. But I tell you, I spit on the idea that that revival should be used as a template. That "revival" died, and in as much as it was a zeal for the *law* of God, it deserved to die.

Fruit unto Hagar. But do you see how all fruit is not created equal? Pastors will take pride in the buildings they erect. Beautiful buildings. Hey, I think God likes beautiful buildings. God likes beautiful. But how many church edifices were built using guilt, or fear, or enticement for more blessings? "Give in order to be more blessed. Get your need met by doing God's work and write out your check. You better at least be giving 10 percent. And if you really want to be blessed, then give more to this project. Take care of God's house and God will take care of yours. Neglect God's house and God will neglect yours." And fabulous church buildings are made off the backs of God's people who are motivated by guilt, or fear or greed or whatever. And people everywhere will point to the buildings and say, "man, what a living church! Look what God's doing there." No! Wrong! Those buildings are nothing more than idolatrous monuments to Hagar! They are fruit born of adultery.

Of course that's not always the case. Certainly not. But constructing a building or even building up a vast congregation is not the determination of success. God is producing perfected fruit in us. Each of us! That is success! As a church, we are successful already.

This is the beauty of having your identity in Christ. As a pastor, I am huge success, not because I do so many wonderful things; but because that's who Jesus made me to be. I know the good news of Jesus, and I know it more and more fully every single day. And I know that I am called to speak it out. And that is the fruit that Jesus bears in me. And it is my joy. And if we would have ten thousand in church, I would be no more successful as a pastor than I am if we would have 15 in church. Success is just intimacy with Jesus, and the fruit that comes out of that.

It's a gift. You're a success today, because you know the good news of Jesus, and you have intimacy with him. You've made it! That's the good life. You're not going to be more of a success next year when you get your degree; or next year when you get your promotion, or next year when the last kid moves out of the house and dog dies. Today is the success of your life because you know the gospel, and you have intimacy. And you're producing fruit unto Jesus, your groom. That's a good life. That is life, right there.

Here's my advice to pastors who are reading this; stop trying to produce fruit in your ministry. And stop trying to produce fruit in your people. But just point people to Jesus. And do one other thing; deal ruthlessly with anything in your worship service that keeps people thinking that something separates them from God. Pastor, stop the confession and forgiveness hamster wheel. (Our church has a confession of righteousness!) Stop telling people that they need to "get their sin under the blood." Cease all practices that contribute to them being sin-focused. Rather, remind them of who they _really_ are. And point them to Jesus and intimacy with him, and then let Jesus produce fruit in your people.

It's telling, because Jesus goes on in his message to the church at Sardis and he talks about people who really do "have it going on." People who are examples in the church and what it is that they possess. Look at verse 4 in our scripture; "*You have a few names even in Sardis who have not defiled their garments; and they shall walk with Me in white, for they are worthy.*"

A few names who have not defiled their garments. Again, the name is the identity. We're talking about identity. People whose identities have not been soiled, or mucked up.

And again, the way it's been preached is that you muck up your garment (you muck up your "Jesus-clothes") by participating in some sin. Your sin is the filth that makes you dirty.

So, people will get a new set of clothes for their baptism in some traditions. That's great. That's wonderful. But there's this song I remember hearing on the radio a few years back about keeping your baptismal clothes clean. So that after you come out of the baptism, you put on your new suit, and the way you keep it clean is by not entering into sin. "I don't want to get mud on my shoes by going somewhere I shouldn't go. Because then Jesus will have to wash me up again." And people inevitably do something they regret in life. And now your baptism suit is mucked up, and "Jesus, please wash my suit again." And people will feel that Jesus forgives them because they came forward at the altar. And then they'll be great for a time, but inevitably will do something again that they regret. And now it's back to the altar. Ad nauseum.

Congratulations! You've just entered the hamster wheel of religion. That suit that you think gets mucked up every time you sin, that suit that you think needs cleaned by Jesus over and over and over again, if you keep washing it, it's going to be thread bear by the time you're dead.

Actually, the garment that Jesus gives is his righteousness. And you cannot muck up his righteousness with anything you do, good or evil. He has already taken your muckiness on himself. The way to a filthy garment is not through *doing something bad*. It's though unbelief. "There are those in Sardis whose names, whose identities, have not been mucked up! But who are doing exactly as I have instructed them from the beginning, they are remembering how they first received righteousness as a gift, and they are keeping on receiving in the same way." There are those who are saying, "I got righteousness as a gift from Jesus ten years ago when I first believed; and today, I have still got my righteousness as a gift from Jesus because I simply believe." The robes on those people are white!

Remember the white I told you about in the last chapter? There's the Greek word for white, *aspros*. It's a common word for the color. That's what you would expect this word to be when Jesus says that these people who have their right identities in him are clothed in white.

Except that Jesus doesn't use that word (*aspros*) to describe the white innocence of his people. He uses the word *leukos*. *Leukos* means dazzling, brilliant white. And the word *leukos* is only used a few times in scripture. It's used to describe Jesus at his transfiguration; when it says that his face and his clothes became brilliant, dazzling white, as no fuller on earth could make them (that kind of white; dazzling white!). That's *leukos*. It's used to describe the white at the resurrection. And it's used when Jesus declares the innocence of the crowd that is coming toward him; he said that they are declared white for the harvest. Jesus declares their innocence for the harvest.

When you look out over a crowd of people, you must see them with the eyes of Jesus. They are not sinners in the hands of an angry God a God who is waiting for them to repent and confess their sin. But Jesus has spoken forth his verdict over them; "Innocent! Innocent!"

Your identity is not just that you are white with innocence. But you are the white of Jesus in his transfiguration. You are transfiguration white. You are resurrection white. White like no human effort, no amount of human bleaching could ever produce. You are supernatural white. You are God's glory kind of white. You are God's righteousness white. And that is the gift that Jesus drapes you in. I tell you, that garment is on your shoulders right now. That is your identity, your true name. Don't believe anything different. To believe anything different is to think that your garment is stained and mucked up.

No, but the people who know their names, Jesus says, "they will walk with me for they are worthy." Your worthiness comes in simply believing your identity. Jesus made you worthy. The fact is, if you don't believe that; if you believe you are unworthy of walking with Jesus, then guess what, you won't. You won't! But those who know their identity; those who know their sonship; the ones who let Papa put the BEST robe on them (the BEST robe was Jesus robe); the ones who let Papa put the best robe on them, the ring on their finger, the shoes on their feet; those who know sonship; *they walk with Jesus.*

Hey, you walk with Jesus. You are worthy. The robe is on you. Walking with him, intimacy with him; that's what life is all about. The fruit that comes out of intimacy with your groom; that makes life good. And he says, verse 5; *and I will not blot out his name from the Book of Life; but I will confess his name before My Father and before His angels.*

This is just beautiful; and I'll end on this thought. People read this about Jesus blotting out the names of people from the book of life. "He's going to blot out your name from the book of life in heaven, and you won't make it in. So watch what you do." No, listen. Jesus said this as an assurance to you against all the people who say stupid things like that. Jesus wants you to know his security. He wants you to know something. This is what he said, *"I will not blot out your name from the book of life.* Forget what other people are telling you. I won't do it. I will not. Your name is in there. And I'm glad it's in there. And I keep it there. I will never remove it. On the contrary," says the Lord; "it's not just that there's some record of your name in some book in heaven; but Papa and I are going to be talking you up all the time. I will confess your name before my Father and before his angels."

Jesus talks to papa about you. He loves bringing up your name. He says things about who you really are. To confess means literally, "to say the same thing as." Jesus speaks out exactly who you are to the Father (exactly who He made you to be), and they talk about you. You know, you talk about what you love. Some people love golf, can't stop talking about golf. Some people love politics; they can't shut up about politics. Jesus loves you. And he can't stop talking about you. How beautiful is that?! Your place is secure. You are clothed in resurrection righteousness. You are intimate with Jesus. He bears his fruit in you, and he and your Papa can't stop talking about how much they love you.

REVELATION
THE CHURCH AT PHILADELPHIA

And to the angel of the church in Philadelphia write, 'These things says He who is holy, He who is true, "He who has the key of David, He who opens and no one shuts, and shuts and no one opens," "I know your works. See, I have set before you an open door, and no one can shut it; for you have a little strength, have kept My word, and have not denied My name. Indeed I will make those of the synagogue of Satan, who say they are Jews and are not, but lie—indeed I will make them come and worship before your feet, and to know that I have loved you. Because you have kept My command to persevere, I also will keep you from the hour of trial which shall come upon the whole world, to test those who dwell on the earth. Behold, I am coming quickly! Hold fast what you have, that no one may take your crown. He who overcomes, I will make him a pillar in the temple of My God, and he shall go out no more. I will write on him the name of My God and the name of the city of My God, the New Jerusalem, which comes down out of heaven from My God. And I will write on him My new name. 'He who has an ear, let him hear what the Spirit says to the churches.'" — Revelation 3:7-13

These words of Jesus are good news. They are good news and blessing! Jesus is blessing you today.

And here we've read Jesus words to the pastor of the church at Philadelphia. And this is the only church where Jesus has nothing negative to say about their ministry. This is such a sweet, sweet word of Jesus.

He begins with these words from verse 7; *"These things says He who is holy, He who is true, He who has the key of David, He who opens and no one shuts, and shuts and no one opens."* That phrase, "he who has the key of David, He who opens and no one shuts and shuts and no one opens;" that is right out of the Old Testament. And any religious Jew who was reading this would know that this comes from Isaiah 22.

Let's just read this, Isaiah 22:22, *"The key of the house of David I will lay on his shoulder, So he shall open and no one shall shut, and he shall shut, and no one shall open."*

It's almost a direct quote, except Jesus is saying; "That's speaking now about me. I am the one who now possesses the key to the house of David." The key to the house of David that is laid on Jesus' shoulder is symbol language for the authority and rule of David. Do you remember when Isaiah prophesies about the messiah, and he says that "the government shall be upon his shoulders? The government is on his shoulders. It means he carries with him all rule and authority. And here it says in Isaiah 22, the key of the house of David is laid on his shoulders. It's just another picture that says the same thing; all authority and rule has been put on Jesus. So you have this image of a king being able to enter anywhere, have access to anything; the right to go and do as he pleases is given to him.

Except Jesus uses this image to make a point; to convey something very particular. It's not just that the government (all power) is given to him. But the power is in the symbol language of a key that opens and shuts, opens permanently and shuts permanently (opens, it says, and no one shuts; that's permanently open; shuts and no one opens, that's permanently shut). So the power of the opening and closing doors has been given to him. And the doors he opens and closes are FOR YOU. They are not for him. They are FOR YOU.

So he says in Verse 8, "*I know your works, See, I have set before you an open door, and no one can shut it; for you have a little strength, have kept my word, and have not denied my name.*"

Jesus has opened a door. For who? For his people! He says, "I have used my authority to open a door (that no one can shut) for you." And he says to them, "Behold this door!"

Look at the verse again; "*I know your works, See, I have set before you an open door.*" The word there for see" is idou, often translated as "behold." Behold; literally, "be perceiving" this. Jesus is saying, "Recognize what is in front of you. There is an open door in front of you."

Now an open door means access. And in this case, you can infer a couple of things. This open door had, at one time, been a closed door to us. Jesus used his authority to open it, *and* he set the door right in front of us, *and* he bids us to make use of it. I mean, the reason he's calling your attention to it is so that you will use it.

Now I'll tell you up front that this is the door of your inheritance in Christ; all of the benefits that we have as sons and daughters of our Father God. That door had been closed, but Jesus has permanently opened it to you. And the way to access those benefits is to know them; to know what Jesus says and what he gives you, and to believe that the door is open for you.

A lot of believers do not "see" (perceive, behold) the open door to their inheritance. They cannot perceive that heaven's door is permanently open to them. They are still trying to get God to open the door of blessing. And they believe that if they ask fervently enough, God will crack the door of heaven open long enough to throw out a couple of nice things before he closes it again. And so we just need to keep asking him, "Please God, please, give me your peace. Please God, I beg of you, please, please forgive me of this sin. Please don't cast me away from your presence."

You know, in the church I came out of, that kind of begging was built into the worship service. And we would say these words that are right out of the Old Covenant (Psalm 51); *"Create in me a clean heart, O God, and renew a right spirit within me, cast me not away from your presence and take not your holy spirit from me."* A believer who says that today is not "seeing" the door that Jesus has permanently opened for them. They don't know that they are clean already, their spirit is perfected forever (they don't need their spirit renewed), God has not cast them away from his presence on account of their sin (the sins of the world were dealt with forever in Jesus) and God is NEVER going to take his Holy Spirit from them; on the contrary, they've been sealed by the Holy Spirit. So why don't they "see" this open door?

Why are some believers able to "see it," and others are not? Here it is. Jesus says that these believers in Philadelphia can "see" this open door; "FOR (because, on account of) *you have a little strength, have kept my word and have not denied my name."*

Three things. One, "They have little strength." Now that does not sound like a positive. But the fact is, they are able to perceive the open door of their inheritance because they are not powerful.

The word for "little" is "micron." We get our word micro from that; teeny tiny. Like a microchip; the tiniest chip available. In fact, it is most often translated as a superlative word; meaning the tiniest amount that is possible and still be existent. So Jesus says, "the mustard seed is the least of all the seeds" (it is the *"micron"* of all the seeds, the smallest seed there is). He says of John the Baptist that no one born of woman is greater than John the Baptist but even the *least* in the kingdom of heaven is greater than him — (again — the superlative meaning). One time the disciples are arguing about, "Who is the greatest." Jesus answers, "him who is *least* in my kingdom, is the greatest." Him who is *"micron"* in the kingdom is the greatest.

So when Jesus says here in Revelation, "You have micron strength," that's a positive. You have the least amount of strength. And I believe he means by that, that they are putting no confidence in their own strength. "You see that your strength is tiny. "You see that you have micro-strength (you have the amount of strength on the farthest, small end of that scale); and that puts you in the place of greatest blessing.

This is the great paradox for those who do not understand God's grace in their life. Those who do not understand God's grace have trouble believing that God's strength is made perfect in our weakness. God's strength is brought to completion when we are people of little strength. Jesus himself said to Paul the apostle, (2 Corinthians 12:9) *"my grace is sufficient for you because my strength is made perfect in weakness." Therefore (Paul says) most gladly will I boast in my weaknesses, that the power of Christ may rest upon me."* Notice that the manifestation of Christ's power RESTS or REMAINS on people who say constantly to God, "I cannot do this in my human strength and I don't have to."

The inability to do something in your human strength puts you in the perfect position to receive God's provision for your life. As long as you believe that you are able; you've no need for God. Curse every teaching that says you can receive from God or accomplish for God or clean up your life for God based on *your* ability or strength.

Think of it this way. If there is some pernicious sin, some stubborn sin in your life, and you want to be delivered and you've never found deliverance for it; the answer for you is not, "try harder this time." It's not "buckle down, get serious and redouble your effort." How many times have you tried that and it hasn't worked. You literally have a history to show that that hasn't worked.

But the church's message to people has been, "get rid of this sin, or else." Get rid of it or else you'll be out of fellowship with God. Get rid of it or you will be cast away from his presence. Get rid of it or the Holy Spirit will be taken from you." No! No! The door to heaven is open by Jesus and no man can shut it, not even you. The threats are all wrong. They are wrong. And how we've been taught to defeat sin is wrong. And church leaders will say, "rely on God to help, rely on God to help." No! Wrong. That's not it.

God does not want to help YOU clean up the old you. Rather, he wants to BE your cleanness. He wants to BE your new life.

You know, it is just right and natural as God's child to want to live a holy life. Someone who doesn't want to live a holy life does not have a revelation of God's love over them or their union with God. But the way to a holy life is not to try hard, even with God's help. The way to a holy life is to enter through the open door of heaven (the door Jesus set before you) and behold Jesus seated on the throne.

The way to holy living is to remove from yourself the misplaced responsibility that says it is up to you and your efforts to clean up your life. You can't do that. You have to recognize that (in yourself) you are a people of micron strength. If you have a revelation of God's love for you, and if you want Jesus to reign and rule in you, then just declare to him, "Jesus, it's all you inside of me. I glory that I do not have any strength to change. I declare myself dead and I declare you to be alive in me." And as you declare that reality of Jesus' life in you, you'll begin to live it. And it won't be you leaving your sin, it'll be your sin leaving you. I am a near expert at this.

Fear clung to me. Depression clung to me. Defeatism clung to me. No amount of pills or resolve or self-help books or even prayer helped. Only beholding Jesus. Only listening to what he said. The thing that helped me most was realizing that I don't have to fix me. And when these things manifested in my life, I didn't have to beat myself up for it, but I simply said, "Jesus, that man who manifested that depression is not the real me. I am a man of micro-strength. I'll stand with you and declare, "that man is dead." Now, tell me who I am. Tell me my real name."

Do you see what I'm saying? The saints in Philadelphia recognized that a door had been opened to them because they put no weight in their own abilities. They counted on Jesus to be their life, to tell them who they were. *"Behold, I have set before you an open door, and no one can shut it, for you have a little strength, have kept my word, and have not denied my name."* You have kept my word. Remember, the word "kept" (Jesus uses it often here in Revelation) means "to guard from loss; to treasure closely." For you to *keep* Jesus' words means that you treasure closely everything that Jesus says about you.

To keep the words of Jesus means that the words of Jesus over you suffer no loss. Walk through the door, behold Jesus and declare; "Jesus, I have micro strength in myself. But I am only who you say that I am. I can do only what you say I can do. So, by your grace, by your divine, unmerited, unearned, influence over me; tell me who I am and what can I do."

And what does Jesus answer? *"You can do all things through Christ who is your strength."* See, if it is no longer you who live, but Christ who lives in you, then everything he is, you are. You are righteous. All the time. You are a son. All the time. You are beloved. All the time. You are pleasing to Papa. All the time. You are worthy of blessings. All the time. (Are you keeping his word? Are you treasuring it up? Are you guarding it from loss?) He says, You are redeemed eternally, perfected forever, sealed by the Holy Spirit. You are delivered from the power of darkness, conveyed into the kingdom of the Son, delivered from the curse of the law, there is now no condemnation for you. (Are you *keeping* his word?) The spirit of him who raised Christ from the dead inhabits your body; you are healed, whole, prospering, and favored. You are qualified to be a partaker of His inheritance. Jesus says, "I have opened the door to blessing. It is open and I have set it in front of you. The door is open and no man can shut it. It is open and not even you can shut it! The door to heaven is open." Are you *keeping* his word?!

See, it's what he says about you. He gives you your identity. He is what is alive in you. It's all, 100%, him, him, him, him, him. Therefore I will glory in my micro-strength! Because when I am weak, it's all him. When I am weak, he's all over that!

And those who get that will be abundantly manifesting God's blessing. You will manifest peace and joy and love and power. And it'll make people jealous who have been trying to work hard for that all their lives. That's what Jesus says in the verse 9, the very next verse. When you finally see the open door to heaven, that all things in heaven belong to you already, then verse 9; *"Indeed, I will make those of the synagogue of Satan, who say they are Jews and are not, but lie, indeed I will make them come and worship before your feet, <u>and to know that I have loved you.</u>"*

This is referring to anyone who is counting on their own strength and their own goodness in keeping the law of God. People who are trying by their efforts to be good enough for God, trying by their efforts to maintain a good position of favor with God; that whole system of trying hard out of the strength of your flesh, that is Satan's system. It's the system that Satan wants you to be stuck in that began in the garden with this lie; "you are not like God. You must do "this" to become like him" (work, work, work, work, work).

"Look at your lack; do this thing, and you'll be like God." It's the system of doing to try to be godly. It focuses on your lack. And believers everywhere are still focusing on their lack. Working, working, working to gain God's approval; still working to be like God.

And you know, what they long for in their heart of hearts is what you already possess. They want peace with God. They want to know that they are acceptable to him, and that he loves them. They want to know that God is pleased with them. You have that already. You received all that as a gift. And so did I. More and more, all the time. And people will look at your joy and your peace and your love that you received through the open door of heaven, they will see you possessing what they don't have; what they have worked for all their lives in vain. And Jesus says here that they'll see it in you and, in the end, they'll come to you for the answer. Why?

Because the blessing rests so heavily upon you. The blessing rests heavily upon those who know the door to heaven is open to them, and who make use of the door every day, every hour.

Jesus has many other wonderful things to say to the church at Philadelphia. Let me just run through a couple of them quickly, because there's one last thing I want to get to that's so beautiful in its imagery.

He says in verse 11, "*Behold, I am coming quickly! Hold fast what you have that no one may take your crown.*" Okay, what do they *have*? The three things. They have a sense of their own weakness in the flesh, they guard from loss Jesus words to them, and they confess Jesus name. So they are not bashful about saying that this is all from Jesus. There is "no other name" for them. That is not exactly politically correct in our day and age, is it? I mean, in our country you can still be pro-God as long as you're not pro-Jesus. The spirit of the last days, says St Paul, is not a spirit of anti-God, it's a spirit of anti-Christ. But we confess his name as the one who has opened everything to us. So Jesus says, "hold fast to that." Why? "*That no one may take your crown.*"

Think about it. The crown is the symbol of authority. The crown is the symbol of reigning and ruling. Believers have been given the crown. We know who we are. We reign on this earth. What we say, goes. When you know who you are in Christ, and you walk into a room, your presence of love and joy and confidence changes the very atmosphere of that room. Your command spoken in the authority of Jesus causes demons to flee and heals broken people. You bind and loose with your words. Now all of that comes by grace. It's all grace. It's all Jesus. The more you understand grace; the more you reign and rule.

Romans 5:17; *"Those who receive the abundance of grace* (how much? — the abundance of grace!) *and the gift of righteousness* (not the working hard to be your own righteousness — but the gift of righteousness) *will reign in life through the One, Jesus Christ."* You might say, "those who receive the abundance of grace and gift of righteousness will wear their crown." And don't let anyone put you back under the system of the law, trying desperately to be "good enough" for God. That will end badly; with you losing your confidence. That will end with you removing your crown.

Now he says in verse 12 these beautiful words. *"He who overcomes, I will make him a pillar in the temple of My God, and he shall go out no more. I will write on him the name of My God and the name of the city of My God, the New Jerusalem, which comes down out of heaven from My God. And I will write on him My new name."*

Jesus says that you get his resurrection name on you, that's your identity. You get your Papa's name on you. That's your identity. You become like God. I am not saying that you *are* God. But we become elevated to a high status. We have been beaten down by condemnation for so long that we have trouble believing that God made us in his image. Yes! He made you in his image. It's not your fault. We are the victims here! We are of the God-kind. Jesus elevated you to take your place with God in the circle of his family. The Bible clearly says that you are seated with Christ in the heavenlies. Seated with the God-Head. Don't put your head down and say, "no, not me, no, no, that can't be." That's what the Bible says. Own it. Treasure that word. Keep it.

That's not a place of turmoil and confusion; it's the place where you find peace being your true self.

Peace is in your identity as a beloved son of God with whom Papa is well-pleased. So we have Jesus' name written on us. We have Papas name written on us. And, Jesus said, he will write on you the name of the city of God, the New Jerusalem. This is so beautiful. Do you know what the name Jerusalem means? *Salem* — you know it better as the word "shalom." Shalom means "peace." *Jeru* means to rain; like water falling from the sky. Jerusalem means *"peace raining down."*

That's your name. Except that it's the *new* Jerusalem. The new way of peace raining down. It is the peace of Jesus. His peace is not as the world gives it. It is not the way everyone tries to get peace; by making everything around them peaceful. No, it's peace that rises up by virtue of your identity. "I am in God, he is in me, he loves me, I am acceptable, he honors me and favors me, God is for me, and if God is for me, who is against me." It's peace that rises from that. Peace raining. That's not just what Jesus gives to you as a gift, but that's what he names you. That's your name. Your name is "Peace rains here!"

And there is so much to say about that, but I want you to see this last thing. Jesus said, *"I will make him a pillar in the temple of My God, and he shall go out no more."* A pillar is a vital, supporting part of the structure in the sanctuary. And the idea here is that you are not just in the temple of God, but that you are that which makes up the temple of God. You are both in the temple, and you are the temple. You are both in God's presence, and he inhabits you. Do you see this in this example?

And here's the beautiful thing. This is like poetry. Because in the beginning of Jesus' words to the church at Philadelphia, he says that he is the one who opens doors that no one can shut and who shuts doors that no one can open. Both of those things. And then he goes on to talk about the door he has opened and set before you, which is access to the benefits of heaven, access to your inheritance.

But what is the door that he has shut? It's right here. Jesus says, I make you a pillar, I put you as a pillar in the permanent presence of Father, "*and you shall go out no more.*" The door is shut to your leaving. He has closed the door and no one can open it again. You are a permanent fixture in the presence of the Lord and he is a permanent fixture in you. And any theology that does not account for this is just wrong. Jesus closed the exit. Once you come to faith in him, there will always be a residual faith in him, I don't' care what comes out of your mouth by way of confession. He made you a new creation, and he does not unmake his new creations. But believer, you are the house of God, and you are in his holy sanctuary. Jesus put you there. You didn't put you there. He put you there. You have found your resting place; and it is in the presence of God, who likes you in that place. And you shall go out no more.

REVELATION
THE CHURCH LAODICEA

"And to the angel of the church of the Laodiceans write; 'These things says the Amen, the Faithful and True Witness, the Beginning of the creation of God: "I know your works, that you are neither cold nor hot. I could wish you were cold or hot. So then, because you are lukewarm, and neither cold nor hot I will vomit you out of My mouth. Because you say, 'I am rich, have become wealthy, and have need of nothing'—and do not know that you are wretched, miserable, poor, blind, and naked— I counsel you to buy from Me gold refined in the fire, that you may be rich; and white garments, that you may be clothed, that the shame of your nakedness may not be revealed; and anoint your eyes with eye salve, that you may see. As many as I love, I rebuke and chasten. Therefore be zealous and repent. Behold, I stand at the door and knock. If anyone hears My voice and opens the door, I will come in to him and dine with him, and he with Me. To him who overcomes I will grant to sit with Me on My throne, as I also overcame and sat down with My Father on His throne. "He who has an ear, let him hear what the Spirit says to the churches." —Revelation 3:14-21

One of the first sermons I ever remember listening to as a child was a sermon on being a lukewarm Christian that was taken from this passage. And I remember so vividly the image of Jesus wanting to vomit people out of his mouth like you would vomit out rotten food. I can truthfully say that that sermon I heard that day shaped me. It shaped how I viewed Jesus. Now I could probably count on one hand the number of sermons I remember from my youth, but isn't it interesting that this sermon would stay with me.

If you Google the words "lukewarm Christians" you will find an unending supply death. I mean an unending supply of guilt and condemnation that leads to death; your death, because the teachings you will find there will lead you to believe that you are separated from God and that Jesus is angry with you. The traditional interpretation of lukewarm-ness is this way; cold is bad (it symbolizes a cold heart toward God), hot is good (because hot symbolizes zeal for God in your doing); and lukewarm-ness is a life that is somewhere between those two things. And this gets directly applied to church-going believers. Because people in church are at least going to church, so they're not cold. 'But . . . . are you doing enough?" That's the question. They're not hot.

So lukewarm Christians go to church, but don't always *want* to go to church. They go, but they *miss* sometimes. They should want to go more. Luke warm Christians read their bibles, but they don't read them enough. "You read it once a day; it should be 3 times a day. It should be more." (This is a great performance enhancing strategy by legalistic preachers, because no matter how zealous you are, no matter where you are on the scale of good works, you should do more! After all, you don't want Jesus vomiting you out). "You aren't praying enough. You aren't evangelizing enough. If you were really hot for God, you would be leading people to Jesus every day. But look at you. You haven't done it. And let's just look at your giving statement from last year; because you gave, but did you give enough? Did you sacrifice? You aren't sacrificing for God's kingdom. You aren't sold out. Where is your zeal for God?"

There are long, long lists of identifiers for Lukewarm Christians; "21 identifiers of a lukewarm Christian;" "18 identifiers of a lukewarm Christian." They "help" you know if you're a lukewarm Christian. And the inherent antidote for lukewarm-ness is to increase your zeal and do more for the kingdom. These are dire warning sermons. Fear inducing sermon. Guilt producing sermons. Angry sermons. Anger is preached out. It's the anger of preachers who both feel God's disappointment over their own lives, and project that disappointment over your life. "If God isn't happy with me, after all I've sacrificed, don't be thinking he's happy with you." Now I'm going to tell you that that whole thing is wrong, and I will show it to you plainly. Today, you will leave these words of Jesus rejoicing, unless, of course, you're a lukewarm Christian. Then you'll hate what I have to say.

But preachers everywhere are saying this; "the church of Laodicea is THE church that represents the modern day church." And I would agree with them. I believe that Laodicea is the modern church. But everything about how we view this church is tied to what Jesus meant by "hot," and "cold," and "lukewarm."

First of all, for those who have jumped right to this chapter with reading the teachings on Revelation, Jesus gives the parameters for interpreting his words to the churches early on in chapter one. So if you miss that, you get everything wrong. Here's the picture. The picture is that of Jesus walking on the earth among all seven of the lampstands (the lampstands represent the seven institutional churches). How does Jesus walk among the seven churches on the earth simultaneously? He does it through his people. Jesus walks on the earth in you and in me. Where you go, Jesus goes.

So what we're really seeing here in Revelation is a picture of Jesus in God's people who are judging these seven ministries; these seven churches. Some of the ministries are doing well. Some need rebuked. Some are just awful and need removed. And Jesus says that he makes a decision to remove the lampstand from its place. That's you, God's people, making the decision to no longer support a church. And you walk away from the church and that church dies; it has it's lampstand removed. So this is Jesus' message to the pastors (*the messengers* — the ones that carry the message); it's Jesus message to them about what they're teaching right, and what they're not teaching right.

Therefore, the first thing to remember when you hear about Jesus wanting to vomit you out of his mouth is that he is not talking about *you*. In fact, he is not talking about ANY believer. Jesus does not do that. He's talking about this institutional church in Laodicea that makes him nauseous when he thinks about what is being preached there.

Now, I've been to the church at Laodicea. This church has many extensions all over the world. I've eaten the food that's being served there from the pulpits and I've had that very same feeling of nausea. "If I could just get what I've heard out of my system; if I could just throw up, I'd feel better!

But the point is; don't let anyone tell you that Jesus wants to spew people out because they're lukewarm. That's not what this is saying.

The issue is that there is something being taught at Laodicea that is affecting the people and causing them to not be intimate with Jesus. Something is being taught that's keeping the people in a place of lack and misery. Verse 17, *"Because you say, "I am rich, have become wealthy, and have need of nothing" and do not know that you are wretched, miserable, poor, blind and naked."*

Okay, there is something below the surface at Laodicea that needs addressing. Jesus starts off with saying, "here is your perception of yourself." You say, *"I am rich, I have become wealth, and have need of nothing."* This is the outward appearance of the believers at Laodicea. It's all about material wealth. And apparently the teaching that was being propagated there was a very familiar teacher in Judaism; that if you have wealth, it means that you are blessed of God. And their whole statement about their identity (how they see themselves) centers on material wealth. "I am rich, I have become wealthy, and have need of nothing."

Well, that Jewish equation; "wealth = the full blessedness of God" is not true. And that teaching has kept them locked in, unable to move forward in thinking more deeply about Jesus.

Jesus shows them the true state of their souls. He says, *"You do not know that you are wretched, miserable, poor, blind and naked."*

Now what I want to show you is that, right here, Jesus has given us a diagnoses of what it means to be lukewarm. I mean, that's the issue, right? This church is teaching and producing lukewarm-ness. What does lukewarm-ness mean? It apparently means, according to Jesus, that (inside, in your heart) you are "wretched, and miserable, and poor, and blind and naked."

Now just think about it. If you are miserable, I'm pretty sure you know it. But if you are convinced that miserable is normal, then "what can you do?" If wretched, miserable, poor, blind and naked is what it means to be a believer, then this is normal. This is the way God wants me, and there's nothing I can do about it. I should rejoice in my misery.

Many people teach that the ideal state of a Christian is misery. They'll call it something else; they'll use other terms that sound more religious. For instance, they'll call it the "way of the cross;" the requirement of your dying to self (not understand that dying to self means dying to your efforts at being made right with God). Or they'll call it *brokenness*; but that's really the same thing as *miserable*. "God wants to keep you broken before him." "I'm just staying broken before God." That sounds so religious, doesn't it? Another word that's used is "humility." "He wants to keep me humble." By *humble* they mean "feeling sorry." Feeling badly for sins which, in their minds, equals teach-ability. What it really translates to is a perpetual state of condemnation. Of course, that's not what *humble* means. Jesus was humble. To be humble means to know your place before God. It means you know who God is and you know who you are in relation to God. That is real humility. But if you think humility is you feeling sorry, you being broken; then you will think that miserable is the normal state in the Kingdom of God.

I believe that this is one of the great lies that has been perpetuated in the church in contemporary music and in preaching and teaching; that staying broken before God is the way to constant fellowship with him. "Break me, O God." No. Jesus came to heal the broken. Jesus doesn't want broken people to remain broken. He wants broken people healed. Jesus said of the Father, *"He sent me to heal the broken hearted."* Someone will ask, *"What about 'a broken and contrite heart, O Lord, you will not despise'"* from Psalm 51. Exactly, an Old Covenant Psalm. You bring your brokenness to God under the law and what does he do with it? He wants to heal it! God wants whole people. He wants healed people. Brokenness is not a virtue. It is part of the curse that Jesus came to heal.

Jesus is looking at the people's brokenness in Laodicea and grieving over it. "This is needless. But you have been taught that it's normal. You don't see how abnormal this is." Look at these words that Jesus uses. He says *you are wretched* — the Greek word behind this is very interesting. It's the word for talent (which is a weight of measure; remember the parable of the talents — they are given a talent of gold). So this is a direct reference to a weight of money that has been "calloused" (literally), it's been added to. It would be likened to our expression that says, "you've come up short in the balance." You've come up short, and you're making it look like you're not. That is *wretched*. That's why Jesus says in the next verse; "buy gold from me. It's purified gold; it is gold that has its full weight about it." I'll get to that in a minute.

Jesus says they are wretched (they are coming up short in their heart! Amen? This is an internal issue), and miserable (they know it, but they think it's normal). Then he says that they are *poor*; literally, "*one who begs.*" That is exactly the word here. *One who begs*. Who are they begging? They're begging God. This is their practice. They think that begging God is normal.

This describes most people in the modern church. Beg God for daily bread. Beg God for forgiveness. Begging God is the normal approach to getting something from God. No. That's normal under the Old Covenant. But that's not how it is in the New Covenant. The New Covenant is *"we have obtained our inheritance"* (past tense — Eph. 1:11). *"The inheritance of Abraham has come upon the Gentiles in*

223

Christ Jesus" (past tense — Gal. 3). *"We have been blessed with every blessing in the heaven places in Christ"* (past tense — Eph. 1:3). No more begging. The door to heaven is open. As believers in the finished work of Jesus, we simply receive what belongs to us already. That's the Christian life. But if you think begging is normal, then that's what you'll do. You'll be a beggar before your Father. Are you getting a taste now of what's being taught in Laodicea?

They are needy (coming up short with God), they are miserable in their hearts, they are begging for what they need, and . . . they are *blind and naked*. Look at those last two things.

They are blind. Now, we've already established that we're not talking about physical blindness. This is a symbol that Jesus is using to identify a problem. What does Jesus mean that they are blind? Jesus used that term often as a symbol in his earthly ministry to designate a spiritual problem. But he used it exclusively, only, applying it uniquely to the blindness of the Pharisees. Matthew 23:16; *"woe to you, blind guides.* Verse 24; *"Blind guides who strain out a gnat and swallow a camel."* (I love that line — they can't abide the easy thing to swallow, the gospel of grace; they'd rather attempt the impossible — swallowing the law of God). "You are dishes that are clean on the outside and filthy on the inside." Verse 26; *"Blind Pharisees, first cleanse the inside of the cup and dish that the outside of them may be clean."* Matthew 15:14; *"They are blind leaders of the blind. And if the blind lead the blind, both will fall into the ditch."* That is Jesus' one and only application of spiritual blindness; his applying it to the Pharisees.

Are you getting it? These are the ones who think that their holiness is determined by their DOING. Those are the ones who are blind. They are the ones who say (Jesus says) "I can see; I can see the way to God. It's by doing lots of good things. It's by my righteous life. My efforts at righteousness." No, that is blindness. It is self-deception. The only way to clean the inside of the cup is to receive the cleaning of Jesus; receiving righteousness as a gift. But what is being taught in Laodicea? They are a community of Christ followers. They believe in Jesus, but they are blind; depending on their own righteousness. Where does that leave them? It leaves them naked in their minds before God; which is the last thing on Jesus' list. It leaves them shamed before God in their minds.

Listen, if you are ever ashamed of coming to God, it's because you are operating out of the mindset of the Pharisees. You are blind to the wonderful way of grace that Jesus has provided you. You think you have to earn God's good attention by your good behavior. That's blindness. You have revealed your inability to see what Jesus has done for you. You think that you have to cover your sin before coming to God. That's blindness. The people in Laodicea were blind. They approach God in shame. "I'm so sorry I did this sin again, O Lord. How can you stand me? How can you forgive me?" Those are the words of blind Pharisees; people who are mixing in the Old Covenant of the Law that was based on you doing; with the New Covenant of grace that comes from belief in Jesus.

Well, there it is.

What is the lukewarm church; the Laodicea church? It is the mixture church. It is the church that mixes together the cold of the stone tablet covenant, with the hot of the New Covenant of grace, the New Covenant of Jesus. "We believe in Jesus, but we are still counting on our own righteousness." And what you get from that mixture are people who think it's normal to be wretched, and miserable, and poor and blind and naked.

Jesus says of that church, of that mixture church, "your teaching makes me nauseous. Look at what it's doing to my people. Look at where it's left them. They don't know what belongs to them. They're walking around still in their nakedness and shame. And they are miserable."

And then preachers everywhere will say, "Oh the solution to your lukewarm-ness is to see how you've blown it, people of God, and get hot for Jesus, start doing more for him. Get sold out for him; give more, pray more, fast more, give more, read your bible more, give more. Did I mention give more?" No, no, a thousand times, no! People propagating that "doing" system; they are the blind leading the blind. And both are falling into the pit.

Jesus' solution to the people of Laodicea who had received this rotten teaching was not: "go out and do more." How ironic it is that preachers everywhere preach that the solution to the lukewarm church is "get fired up and do more, get serious about your walk." But Jesus never offers that as the solution. Jesus says, "Let me spend time with you, I will tell you who you are. *"Behold,"* Jesus says TO BELIEVERS, "*I stand at the door and knock, if anyone hears my voice and opens the door, I will come in to him and dine with him and he with me."* Jesus says, "We will sit around the table and talk. And I will tell you who you are." Jesus' solution to lukewarm-ness was not "do more. Increase your doing." It was, "listen to what I say about you." And Jesus' solution is spelled out so clearly, (so clearly!) in the next verse (verse 18) but so many preachers don't preach Jesus' solution, because we sure don't want to let the Bible get in the way of what we preach!

Jesus is trying to undo the damage here in his people from mixture teaching. If the first sermon that I can remember was a mixture teaching on this passage, he's got a lot of undoing to do. All my adult life I was wretched, begging God, begging (because I knew I wasn't worthy to receive from his open hand. I had to negotiate with God; "If you do this God, I will do this over here for you, Lord; I will sacrifice for you"). That is a life of unworthiness. A life of misery. That is the result of a mixture message. It leaves you lacking all the time before God. It leaves you relating to God based on your doing. Letting your good deeds or bad deeds dictate how pleased God is with you today. And (this is the heart of it!) it leaves you feeling the shame of your misdeeds. That's what Jesus means when he talks about the shame of our nakedness. We want to cover ourselves with our doing. We want to be able to say to God, "at least I did this for you. See? A little fig leaf." And all the while we know that it is not enough. When will it be enough?! When will you do enough to cover your nakedness?! Never! Never! Never! Stop trying.

You have to get something, you see, that does not come by your efforts. You have to get something that only Jesus can give you. Verse 18 — *"I counsel you to buy from me gold refined in the fire, that you may be rich, and white garments, that you may be clothed, that the shame of your nakedness may not be revealed, and anoint your eyes with eye salve, that you may see."* See what? See Jesus. See what he's purchased for you. Gold refined in the fire. Interesting, it's not *silver* refined in the fire. Silver is the metal that symbolizes man.

The Old Testament says that human beings are refined as silver in the fire. Refined by trials. And preacher's everywhere will be preaching that you need to be refined in the fire of trials and sacrifices. That's how you get yourself pure. "Bring on the fire, God." No. That was purity under the law; as silver is purified. What Jesus gives is *gold*, the metal of God; the metal that represents God. *He* went through the fire. *He* went through the trial and *he* became the sacrifice. And he *gives* to you the result of his work; the full weight of his redemption! Paid in full. Nothing lacking here. No fudging on the payment.

You are fully redeemed! And the inheritance that he purchased for you, every good thing for your life, is now in your possession. See it! You are rich. Say it now; "I am rich. Everything I need has been given to me by Jesus."

He says, "And I give to you white garments that you may be clothed, that the shame of your nakedness may not be revealed." This is the gift of his righteousness. And this is so important to get. We need reminded of this so often; because without righteousness (which literally means –"the right to"; righteousness means, "the right to" something) without righteousness, we feel unworthy to receive anything from God. Without the righteousness of Jesus that he gives to you as a robe to cover your nakedness, you will feel unworthy and you will not be persuaded that God wants to give you anything. You see, the solution for being a beggar is righteousness. You have a right to your inheritance.

That's why Jesus says that the robe he gives you is *leukos* white. Remember *leukos* white? *Leukos* is not normal white. It is dazzling white. It is transfiguration white, resurrection white (the same word for white used in those places is the word Jesus uses here). White as no fuller on earth, no amount of bleaching, no amount of working on your part to get clean; brilliant, dazzling white. That is the white of your robe. Put it on. See it on you. It's his righteousness that covers your nakedness. It covers your sense of not doing enough. It makes you worthy. Christ is your worthiness. The more you know that, the easier it is to receive your inheritance. You're not disqualified from anything because of sin. You are qualified! You are.

I'll tell you how innocent you are. You must receive this by faith. Jesus is described by John the Baptist as the Lamb of God who takes away the sins of the entire world. When John said that, he was really saying that the entire sacrificial system under the Old Covenant was just a picture of Jesus. That the lamb of sacrifice was a picture of Jesus who would permanently, with one sacrifice of himself, remove every single sin that ever was, and every single sin that ever would be; he would take those sins upon himself, and he would give to you his innocence.

Under the Old Covenant, you would find the lamb of sacrifice to atone for your sin. And that lamb, by symbol, would become your sin. And you, by symbol, would receive the innocence of the lamb.

And this is a picture of the innocence that would get transferred to you. You became as the lamb. What was the lamb like? The lamb, by its very nature, could not participate in the sin that you committed. It was innocent in that way. And it had innocence in that it could not even comprehend the sin. You could not explain the sin to it in a way that the lamb could ever comprehend. But it's not just innocent in its lack of sin, or its lack of understanding, but it is innocent by its *very design*. It is innocent by its very being; in the very kind of being that it is. It can have nothing whatever to do with the sin in which you participate.

And at the time of sacrifice, the offending person would lay their hands on the head of the lamb and confess their sin over that lamb, and then that lamb would be sacrificed as atonement for that sin. The guilt of your sin and, in fact, the very sin itself, got transferred to that lamb so that it was not upon you. And the other thing that happened is that the innocence of that lamb, what the lamb possessed, got transferred to you. That lamb, not just innocent because it didn't participate in your sin, but the very nature of the lamb, the innocence by nature that it possesses in it's being (it's very inability to even comprehend sin) THAT innocence, that purity got transferred onto the person.

And multiplied to the billionth power, The Lamb of God, Jesus, your Lord, took every sin that ever has been done, and every sin that ever will be done upon himself. He who knew no sin (who did not ever participate in sin; but more than that, who could not comprehend sin by virtue of his very being) he took your sin upon himself, and he gave to you his full innocence, innocence *in being*, innocence *by design*.

And you are not just in a perpetual state of forgiveness before God. You are not as one who is simply forgiven forever, but Jesus has transferred to you, has given to you as a gift, and you possess right now, at this moment, the very innocence of Christ's nature; that which cannot *by its being* EVER be party to sin. It does not comprehend it. It is only innocence. That is now the gift that he wraps you in as a robe. The depth of your innocence before God is something for you to swim in. That is your innocence. Your true you, your spirit you can no longer comprehend sin. That's why John the apostle said that believers *cannot sin.* This is the nature of your spirit. Your spirit before God retains innocence perpetually. That is not just how he sees you. That's who you really, really are; that is your true self. That is the *leukos* white of the robe that is around you. You are worthy. You are worthy! It covers your nakedness. It covers your shame. There is no shame now before God.

Only peace. Only love. Only joy. Look at you! His glory (that's his nature) surrounds you as a robe, and it has become *your* glory; Jesus residing in you. What does that mean? It doesn't just mean that you are worthy to receive your inheritance. It means more. Much more. He calls you to take your place at the table of the God! You are elevated to the place of fellowship with the Godhead. Verse 21, "*To him who overcomes*" (overcomes what? This abusive anti-Christ mixture teaching!); *"to him who overcomes, I will grant to sit with me on my throne, as I also overcame and sat down with my Father on His throne."* You have a place at the table of God. To talk about anything. To understand your identity. To reign in this life.

CPSIA information can be obtained
at www.ICGtesting.com
Printed in the USA
BVOW09s0718271017

498816BV00017B/250/P